create

con

nect

EXCELLENT
Wow!
Yes

brilliant

Great!

convince

3 in 1

create connect convince

Fundamentals of Advertising • Branding • Communication

Jörg Dietzel

Marshall Cavendish Business

VISUAL CONCEPT & DESIGN: Lock Hong Liang
ILLUSTRATIONS: Bruce Chin and Gao Feng
PHOTO CREDITS: Photolibrary (cover, inside back cover, p 2),
Stephanie Leuker (p 3), Tijmen Van Dobbenburg (inside front cover),
www.sxu.hu (inside back cover)

First published in 2008 by Marshall Cavendish Business
An imprint of Marshall Cavendish International (Asia) Private Limited
A member of Times Publishing Limited
Times Centre
1 New Industrial Road
Singapore 536196
T: +65 6213 9300 / F: +65 6285 4871
E: genref@sg.marshallcavendish.com
Online bookstore: www.marshallcavendish.com/genref

Other Marshall Cavendish Offices:
Marshall Cavendish Ltd. 5th Floor, 32–38 Saffron Hill, London EC1N 8FH • Marshall Cavendish Corporation. 99 White Plains Road, Tarrytown NY 10591-9001, USA • Marshall Cavendish International (Thailand) Co Ltd. 253 Asoke, 12th Flr, Sukhumvit 21 Road, Klongtoey Nua, Wattana, Bangkok 10110, Thailand • Marshall Cavendish (Malaysia) Sdn Bhd, Times Subang, Lot 46, Subang Hi-Tech Industrial Park, Batu Tiga, 40000 Shah Alam, Selangor Darul Ehsan, Malaysia

National Library Board Singapore Cataloguing in Publication Data

Dietzel, Jörg.
create, connect, convince: fundamentals of advertising, branding, communication / Jörg Dietzel. – Singapore: Marshall Cavendish Business, c2008.
p. cm.
Includes index.
ISBN-13 : 978 981 261 626 5
ISBN-10 : 981 261 626 8

1. Advertising. 2. Branding (Marketing) 3. Communication in marketing. I. Title.

HF5823
659.1—dc22 OCN229276651

Printed by Fabulous Printers Pte Ltd

Ingredients

How this book works

There are four main parts to this book:

1. The content narrative

For people (about to start) working in Advertising—whether agency-side or client-side —and students in Advertising, Mass Communication or Promotional Management, this section gives an overview of agency life, its structure and the process of creating communication. It looks at the different media and their roles in today's cluttered market. This part can be read as a narrative for a general overview, or referred to when the need arises.

2. The case studies

We were fortunate to be able to gather some cases on international brands in Asia to illustrate the use of media and ideas to get the message across. Born out of offices in Seoul, Shanghai, Singapore and Manila, these cases are proof that Asian creatives are not in the shadows of their overseas colleagues when it comes to great ideas, surprisingly executed.

3. Friends of Jörg

I thought it would be interesting to have different voices in this book—insights from agency practitioners in Asia and beyond. So I have asked my friends in the industry to contribute. They are:

Sir John Hegarty

Founder of Bartle Bogle Hegarty, the immensely successful London-based agency that created memorable campaigns for Audi, Levi's and Coke. I had the privilege of working with John for three years in London and was impressed by his creativity, personality and humility.

Tham Khai Meng

Co-chair of Ogilvy Asia, and Creative Guru based out of Singapore, Tham helped build Ogilvy into the highly-awarded No 1 network in Asia. He talent-scouts for his offices across the region and is very active in the community at large.

Max Mak

My account director at BBDO Hong Kong, Max has worked in the city for many years, looking after some of the biggest clients in the region and managing account management teams. I have always been impressed by his people skills, and how he motivates his people and builds strong relationships with clients.

Wilson Chow

Wilson was my Creative Director in Shanghai when I ran DDB China. Very passionate and knowledgeable about everything creative, he created the award-winning 'Ants' campaign for Budweiser in China. I persuaded him to go with me to the new DDB Berlin in 2000. Now a top creative at Ogilvy Beijing, Wilson looks after Motorola and other big clients in China.

Andrew Lok

Andrew was a senior writer at Batey when I joined them in 2001. We used to meet during Friday night drinks on the rooftop, and we have collaborated ever since. Andrew helped me develop my company's CI (corporate identity), wrote my wedding invitation and together we won the BMW China account for BBDO/Interone in 2004. Now with Ogilvy in China, he's been my creative inspiration since 2001.

Peter Smyth

Originally from Canada, Peter joined BBDO Hong Kong as head of planning when I was working there. Insightful about Asian consumers, he has been a source of advice ever since. He now works with I&S BBDO Japan.

David Guerrero

Head of BBDO Guerrero-Ortega in Manila, David is one of the leading creatives in Asia. Educated in the UK, he presents creative ideas that clients just buy into. He is, frequently, a chairman of creative juries in Asia and abroad.

Term Shon

Term, of German-Korean origin, joined my Berlin team as a writer and quickly rose to fame, creating award-winning ads for Volkswagen. Now a Professor for Visual Design in Seoul, he shuttles between Berlin and Korea.

Jimmy Liang

An award-winning 'suit' who was also the best man at my wedding, Jimmy was born in Beijing and educated in Hong Kong. He ran DDB Guangzhou during my time in China and built some solid client relationships as well as fathered some great campaigns for Wrigley's in China (based out of Leo Burnett). He now looks after Cadillac in Shanghai.

Neil French

I was lucky to get Neil French (introduced by Lim Sau Hoong) to write the foreword to my book. Neil is probably the world's most famous creative director, having created memorable campaigns for decades in Asia, Europe and the US. He is also well-known for his irreverent style. His 10-year-old video, "The Good and The Great", is still a must-see for every advertising class.

4. The characters

In order to illustrate the process of agency-client relationship—from first pitch to final product on air—we invented a Beijing agency, some quirky characters and their quest to advertise "Happy Jelly". Exaggerated? Sure. Stereotypical? Maybe. But we hope it is also an indication that working in communication can—despite the long hours, low pay and human drama—be a lot of fun!

Notes on case studies

Audi / formul8

A good example of a print campaign developed not for the brand owner but for the local importer. The agency had to strike a balance between tactical messages (the importer is in the business of selling cars) and building the brand.

Australia Tourism / M&C Saatchi

For a long time, all tourism campaigns were similar, showcasing the landmarks of the country they advertised. Then M&C came along with a different idea: Show the landmarks that tourists need to see, but combine them with witty copy and a provocative outcry. A good case of calculated provocation, the "Where the bloody hell are you?" line drew global attention and numerous editorials—priceless.

Dove / Ogilvy

A truly integrated campaign that challenges industry convention and pays tribute to a new, more honest way of communicating. The "Campaign for Real Beauty" shows that beauty is indeed in the eye of the beholder and aims to relieve some of the pressure, especially for young girls, to conform. Across media, and locally adapted for more relevance, it is a good example of advertising blazing new trails and riding global trends.

FedEx / BBDO

Call me biased (I worked on this campaign for almost three years), but the "We live to deliver" campaign in Asia-Pacific does everything a campaign should do: It manages to position FedEx clearly, differentiates it from the competition, and is memorable and fun to watch.

I Love This Ad / Term Shon
Professor Term Shon found these stickers which popped up on outdoor billboards in Berlin and Seoul a few years ago. An interesting example of how emancipated consumers now have a voice (not just online) and 'talk back'.

Kinetic / Kinetic
Sometimes a 'self-ad' works best to showcase an agency's talents. Kinetic developed a website for themselves that is not only an impressive touchpoint—it also works as a reference for what the agency can do for its clients.

Singapore Navy / Saatchi & Saatchi
A great example of how a Direct Mailer with an idea can indeed cut through the clutter, reach its target and work as a call to action. Saatchi successfully managed to find an insight into the target group (they were looking for adventure and excitement) and, by contrasting an ordinary life with a life in the navy, created a high response rate.

Tamiya Car / Creative Juice/G1
Thailand is famous for its quirky humour—in this case, it's the simple idea of using a "breaks into many pieces" analogy that gets the message across in a new, surprising and memorable way. Not unexpected from this much sought-after creative 'hotshop' that—despite being part of the TBWA network—has managed to hold on to its independence and quirkiness.

Tiger Beer / Leo Burnett
"A big brand needs big advertising", an APB executive once said to me. Faced with the challenge of different perceptions at home and abroad, Tiger tasked Leo Burnett to come up with a 'big idea' which resulted in this exciting series of ads, based on a product differentiator: The medals the beer has won for decades, which translate into 'quality'.

adidas / TBWA
Outdoors is probably where the medium has the biggest leeway for new, unusual ideas. Who says billboards can only take ads? In this one, the agency made it come alive and created global PR value way above the client's advertising budget.

Acknowledgements

I would like to thank all my friends who helped me write this book—by encouraging me to start in advertising, stay in advertising and start out on my own after 15 years in advertising.

Gerhard Koepp was my first boss at DAMM and he taught me all about client management. Bernard Brochand supported me at DDB and sent me places; Keith Reinhard and John Bradstock gave me some tremendous opportunities. John Hegarty told me all about creativity, and how to evaluate ideas. Andrew Lok has been a good friend and creative source from the beginning on Batey's roof, and we have proven that, as a team, we're unbeatable. Sir Martin helped in my move to Singapore and still has an open ear and words of wisdom for me. Wilson and Jimmy worked with me at DDB China—we had lots of fun and became friends for life. Max helped me run FedEx, ran the team at BBDO and is a constant support. Peter is living proof that you can be a successful strategic planner and nice; Term went a long way from Art Director in Berlin to Professor in Seoul.

I have been blessed to have been able to work with some of the best creative minds in the world: John Hegarty in London, Andy Berlin in New York, Tham Khai Meng in Singapore, Thirasak in Bangkok, Lim Sau Hoong at 10AM and David Guerrero in Manila. They are living proof that Asia does not lag behind the West when it comes to ideas.

I have also been lucky to work with understanding, daring, supportive clients: Jose at OPRC, Malcolm, Michael and Shelly at FedEx, and everybody at Audi in Ingolstadt and Singapore.

Many agencies have helped and supplied cases for this book, foremost of which is my friend Fiona and her team at formul8; also M&C Saatchi, TBWA, Kinetic, Ogilvy, Creative Juice\G1, Saatchi & Saatchi and Leo Burnett. Thank you all.

I am privileged to have Neil French contribute the foreword—like everybody else, I have been an admirer of his for some time and am still showing the excellent 'Good to Great' video to my students.

And thanks to Bruce Chin (for Goh Chwee Noi), my trusted Teaching and Research Assistant, without whose help this book would not have been possible.

Finally, thanks to my parents who have always encouraged me to 'be who I want to be'.

Author's note

Recently, I watched a movie about how a rediscovered hero from the 60s helped a young policeman, played by Keifer Sutherland, reconnect with his past. It made me reflect on the values of the 60s generation, and I wondered how many of those values were experiencing a renaissance today.

Subsequently, I wrote an article entitled 'Flower Power's Final Victory,' which was published in both Hong Kong's *Media Magazine* and German magazine *brand eins*. The article traced the emergence of the new, emancipated consumer: One who is more confident of his ideas and is capable of critical thinking when deciphering advertising and branding messages; one who is more empowered by creative thinking and better able to express his unique point of view. I had noticed some examples of such creative expression in Seoul and Berlin where stickers on outdoor billboards, presumably stuck on by pranksters, read "I [heart] this ad" or "I [puke] this ad." The younger generation is also extremely skilled in developing its own content on video hosting websites such as YouTube and MySpace, with or without the consent of featured brand owners.

This creative expression is a movement that started in the West, but it is gaining popularity here in Asia. Its growth has become too important to ignore, and the existence of the new, emancipated consumer must make us relook the way we communicate our brands and products. Today, we are being challenged to overcome the doubt—and often cynicism—of the modern consumer by harnessing and encouraging his creativity and engaging him with interactive media.

Brands that understand these challenges and are willing to come up with new ways of communicating more honestly and creatively are more likely to gain acceptance and loyalty among the new consumer generation in Asia as well as across the globe. I will talk more about the implications of this trend at the end of this book.

Of course, many of the old rules still apply. This book will look into all aspects of communication and brand building, exploring 'old' as well as 'new' media, 'above', 'below' and 'through the line'. However, it will also look into why and how the changing mindset of the new consumer should influence the ways in which these old and new tools are applied. In short, it will attempt to explain what being mindful of 'Flower Power's Final Victory' means.

Jörg Dietzel

The Legian, Bali, 2008

Foreword

Why would you read this little piece?

This book is full of marvellous observations, and splendid advice, from all manner of industry worthies. What could I possibly add which would be anything other than repetition?

So, I'll keep it simple.

Amid all the talk about the changing face of the media universe, and the bewildering plethora of technical whim-whams, designed, it might seem, to make the job of the creative chap or chapess even more confusing ... and with the correlation that this allows even more people to give their opinion about why you're wrong ... one truth remains.

However you are delivering your message, and in whatever medium you are doing so, and however brilliant your grasp of the arcane skills involved, the only person that matters is the one to whom your message is addressed.

The single person.

Not 'the audience'. Not 'the market'. Not even the 'market segment'.

You must KNOW this person. The only research that is of the slightest use to you is that which throws more light on that one living, breathing, entity.

One other Great Truth is that this poor benighted human being not only doesn't care what you have to say, but generally detests the way it impinges on his life. As I write this, I have one eye on a Formula One race; Raikkonen has just stuffed his Ferrari into the tyre-wall at 150mph ... and at this point some clown believes that I really need to know how to get a shave that will attract babes. (I hope an exclamation mark would be superfluous.)

Just remember that what you have to say, and the way you say it, has to compete with and surpass whatever is on the screen or the page you have the temerity to interrupt.

There will be dozens of people clamouring to explain that the message needs to conform to this or that template; that the tagline/logo needs to be emphasised.

There'll be platoons of jobsworths queuing up in their capacity of official mind-readers, to tell you that the client won't like it.

Remember that these poltroons have only one interest close to their hearts: their own survival.

But when you know you're right, you are right, and everyone else is wrong. This may get you fired, in which case you have the opportunity to work somewhere else. Or take up a different career. But it is YOUR career; YOUR life.

Don't live that life for someone else.

That's all.

Neil French
2008

Hi, I am Xiao Mei. I live in Beijing. After graduation, I was really lucky to find a job as an Account Executive at a multi-national corporation (MNC) ad agency, BDDA. I started a week ago, and am very excited.

Hi, I am Mr. Wang. I own a small factory in Tientsin. We produce sweet jelly—in different colours and flavours —as a sweet. It's called "Happy Jelly". We need to build a brand, in order to compete with the multinationals. That's why I have engaged BDDA.

Hi, I am Ping Ping—GM of BDDA Beijing. I am from Singapore, but have lived in China for four years now. We have just won the "Happy Jelly" account—such hard work! We had to go through four rounds and spent so many nights in the agency. But finally we got it—thanks to our strategic thinking. I think.

CAMPAIGN TITLE

CAMPAIGN FOR REAL BEAUTY

CLIENT

Unilever - Dove

AGENCY

Ogilvy & Mather Asia Pacific

AGENCY CREDITS

Account – Yan Yi Chee
Creative – Christen Monge
Planning – Benoit Wiesser

TIME FRAME OF CAMPAIGN

June 2005 – November 2005

CAMPAIGN TITLE

Campaign For Real Beauty

OBJECTIVES OF CAMPAIGN

As a personal care brand with a rich heritage, Dove has always stood for the beauty of real women and the wholesome care qualities of its unique ¼ moisturising milk. But as it stood on the eve of an unprecedented expansion into new segments and higher-value categories (the key business objective), the brand needed to carve for itself a powerful and differentiated beauty positioning as a platform for growth. The key marketing objectives were to establish such a re-positioning for the brand and strengthen brand affinity. The communication objectives, in line with the brand's mission of 'Making more women feel more beautiful every day', were to challenge existing definitions of beauty and foster a social debate around the definition of beauty and the pressures women are under to live up to the stereotypical beauty ideals promoted by the media and conventional beauty marketing.

TARGET GROUP

The Dove brand was primarily aiming to engage women who, looking at the unremitting formula of images that the media spew out of perfect —almost cloned—women (flawless fair-skinned, slim young models, with long straight hair and absent expressions), feel distant and removed from them. Yet they are not consciously aware of it. Beyond that, the Dove brand wanted to engage key opinion leaders / experts and indirect targets, e.g. the media, men, teenage girls; as well as internal audiences and trade partners as each has a role to play in a woman's daily experience of beauty.

PROPOSITION

Beauty comes in all shapes and sizes—you don't have to conform to beauty stereotypes to be beautiful.

COMMUNICATION STRATEGY

Due to the unique nature of the brief (vs conventional product-focused campaigns), the approach had to be highly disruptive and able to engage audiences in a genuine two-way dialogue / debate.

A fully-integrated campaign was developed.

- 'Tick-Box' posters in OOH (out-of-home advertising) to debunk prevailing beauty stereotypes and showcase the stunning beauty of real women.
- Provoke and feed a broad social debate about prevailing definition of beauty and its impact on women's self-esteem.
- Leverage on non-conventional media to foster interaction and social debate, e.g. interactive billboards; online discussion boards; coffee-shop collaterals, etc.
- Position Dove as an authoritative expert and a change agent; supported by the publication of a White Paper study, 'The Truth about Beauty in Asia', in partnership with leading academic experts.

CHOICE OF MEDIA

OOH (including interactive billboards to allow for mobile phone voting): social statement; trigger for PR

- PR: TV, mainstream press, beauty press
- Internet: discussion forum
- In-store

CREATIVE EXECUTION

- Series of 6 OOH posters—each focusing on a specific stereotype / beauty issue relevant to an Asian audience, e.g. body shape, age, skin tone, eyes, hairstyle, etc.
- Features real women (ie. not professional models) selected for being beautiful despite not conforming to prevailing beauty ideals.
- Tick-Box device as the optimum solution for the task.
- Intrinsically embodies alternative points-of-view and frames a 'debate.'
- Actively engages viewers to reconsider and take a stand.

COUNTRIES COVERED

Global campaign—adapted for Asia
Japan, Korea, Taiwan, China, Hong Kong, Vietnam, Thailand, Malaysia, the Philippines, Singapore, Indonesia.

RESULTS

- Campaign reached in excess of 299,000,000 consumers
- PR value in excess of $3.1m
- Campaign awareness (total population): Japan 12%, the Philippines 30%, Singapore 19%, Korea 51% (prompted)
- Strong message / issue take-out

Japan

- 81% of those who were aware of the campaign endorsed the statement that 'Dove believes that beauty comes in different shapes, sizes, ages and skin tones' vs only 52% of those who were not aware.
- 50% increase in 'Appeals more than other brands' attribute. (Brand Health Check)

Singapore

- 74% endorsed that 'Dove wants to challenge existing opinions on beauty'.
- 62% agreed with 'Made me think Dove is really different from other brands'.
- 57% agreed with 'It made the brand more appealing'.

The Philippines, ABC Women

- 39% strongly agreed with 'Makes me think beauty comes in different shapes, colours and ages'.
- 38% strongly agreed with 'It reminds me all women can be beautiful'.
- 35% strongly agreed with 'It gives me a different view of beauty'.
- 73% believe the campaign 'Improved their opinion of Dove a bit / a lot'
- 39% strongly agreed with 'Dove is in touch with people like me'.
- 37% strongly agreed with 'Dove is a brand for me'.
- Strong impact on brand affinity.

Malaysia

- 70% agreed with 'Made me think Dove is really different from other brands'.
- 67% agreed with 'It made me think differently about the brand'.
- 73% agreed with 'It made the brand more appealing'.

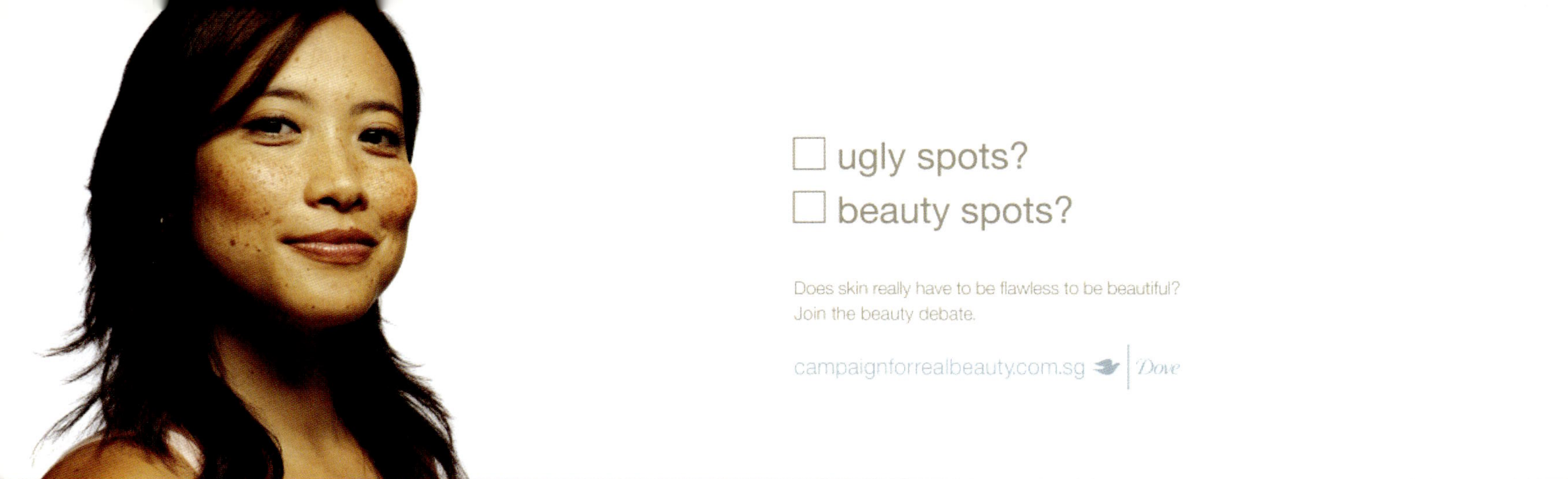
☐ ugly spots?
☐ beauty spots?
Does skin really have to be flawless to be beautiful?
Join the beauty debate.
campaignforrealbeauty.com.sg
Dove

☐ boy?
☐ babe?
Is hair length a true measure of beauty? Join the beauty debate.
campaignforrealbeauty.com.sg
Dove

☐ single eyelids?
☐ twice as nice?
When surgery adds an extra eyelid, does it remove your identity?
Join the beauty debate.
campaignforrealbeauty.com.sg
Dove

☐ grey?
☐ gorgeous?
Why can't more women feel glad to be grey?
Join the beauty debate.
campaignforrealbeauty.com.sg
Dove

Dove
campaignforrealbeauty.ph
aging? 46 %
ageless? 54 %
Text Dove I vote <your choice> to 3993

Dove
flat?
49 %
flattering?
51 %
Text Dove I vote <your choice> to 3983

1. So, you want to communicate?

This book follows the sequence of developing an advertising campaign from start to end. Along the way, we will look at old and new ways of communicating as well as the processes, ideas and technicalities involved in media and production. So, you're working for a brand owner and you want to communicate. But wait a minute—how well do you know the brand? It's in your best interest to make sure that your positioning is relevant and differentiated. Otherwise, even the best advertising campaign cannot convince your target audience to try your product or service. First, you need to consider ...

BRAND BUILDING

Before you make any decisions about your positioning, you need to ask yourself: What can I base my decision on? Too often, positioning decisions are based on assumptions about consumer behaviour and desires as well as the positioning space that you'd like to own. In most cases, the assumptions about consumers are unverified, and the desired positioning is arrived at without considering whether it is already taken or an attractive proposition to your target group. Good decisions can only be made in the face of credible information. So before you start, you will need to determine:

Who Is Your Target Group?

After many years of consultancy work, I am still amazed to see how rarely marketers know enough about their target group. It is vital that you look at your product or service and determine whom it is aimed at, i.e. what kind of people are you trying to reach? You need to know what they are like, how they live. This information is important for insights into the media consumption habits of your target group, and it will help you to choose the right channels of communication. You should also be familiar with their needs, dreams and aspirations in order to get an idea of how to position your brand and determine the kind of message you want to send. The bottom line is that you need to know exactly whom you're aiming your brand at. Sometimes, it helps if you write up detailed descriptions of imaginary target consumers and give them real names. In this way, creative teams will have an easier time imagining whom they are talking to and can thus be more focused in deciding what tone of voice to use.

Once you have determined who your target is, you can embark on the big information search. We call this the:

BRAND AUDIT

It is not an audit in the usual sense where men in grey suits with clipboards and calculators invade your office and occupy the conference room for a few weeks. This audit looks into the available secondary research sources such as online surveys, published consumer reports or press clippings, and supports these with some primary research in the market. Here are some areas a brand audit would look at:

Your Target Group

What other details can you find out about the target group? If you're already in the market, what do they know and think about your brand? If you're a startup, what expectations and attitudes do they already hold for services or products in your category? What influences their decision? Is it price, status or brand?

Understanding the factors that play a role in their decision-making process allows you to come up with a solution that will best fit their needs. You also need to consider the potential barriers that will prevent your target group from trying your offer so that you can think of marketing and communications solutions to overcome these.

The Market / Segment

Which segment of the market do you belong to? Is this segment growing or shrinking? How crowded is it? What are the trends that you need to know? Who are the competitors? How are they positioned? What are the segment conventions and should you follow or disrupt them? Where is the 'white space' on the competitive map that you can own? What gives you reason to believe your product or service would be attractive to consumers? What are your reasons for occupying that 'white space?' Could there be a reason why it is still blank?

As for your competition, whom are you really competing with? By now, almost everybody would have read Kim and Mauborgne's bestselling *Blue Ocean Strategy* and many would be wanting to create their own blue ocean. Your competitors are probably seeking to create a new market segment of their own.

However, while there is some merit in that idea, it is an approach that looks at the situation a little too much through the eyes of the manufacturer. That's because, from a consumer's viewpoint, there is always a choice. You may think your new resort in Bali is different enough to create a new segment, that it is more than just a hotel or resort. Yet the consumer looking for a luxurious break may hold you in comparison to other more conventional accommodation options such as the Four Seasons Sayan or Uma Ubud. Or perhaps, after a successful business deal, they may be looking at the market for some other form of reward. If this is the case, your luxury getaway then has to compete with a Harley Davidson motorbike or an Ikepod watch.

The lesson here is to be aware of the way your target group thinks and view your competition accordingly.

Megatrends

A few years ago in Singapore, I watched the amazing American trend expert Faith Popcorn point out some worldwide megatrends that had started in the West but were beginning to see the light in Asia. Today, these trends are conquering the world and are what I would call human megatrends. They are not limited to a specific segment or market and are instead based on shifts in human technology, thus influencing every market and segment in most countries of the world.

For example, the global health trend is growing stronger each year and shows no sign of stopping. What does that mean for your resort, the materials of the clothes you produce or the recyclability of the car you build? The emancipated consumer of today is looking at companies for responsibility; having a great product at a good price is no longer enough because the new consumer is interested in factors such as how the brand owner treats his staff and the environment. Faith refers to this as SOS, which stands for Save Our Society, an expectation of responsibility that was previously only expected of the government, but which is now directed at manufacturers.

You need to be aware of megatrends—there are many around, and sometimes they are contradictory—for they may affect your brand.

Once you have done your homework, what do you do with all the data you have collected? You follow the economist's motto: Simplify, then exaggerate. Obviously, you need to make sense of all the numbers, so you need to carry out a careful management summary that lists the most important findings about the target, the market, the competition and the trends. That should give you a pretty good picture about what's going on, so you can use this as a basis for your:

BRAND POSITIONING

Basically, this is the process of figuring out what you're all about. Let's digress for a moment and look at a simple analogy for brands that I always use in my first class with a new group of students:

In the middle is the Brand Core or your DNA. This is what makes you who you are. Your name would be part of that. It also determines whether you're male or female and is influenced by your heritage, ethnicity, sexual orientation and your convictions, opinions and values. The Brand Core is everything that makes you, you. This core would normally be pretty stable once you have reached a certain age. While you may decide to reposition your brand by changing your opinions or going for a sex change for example, at the core, you will still be who you are and will largely remain the same.

But like a brand, you will have target groups that you need to communicate with, that you will want to have a certain opinion of who you are and what you stand for. These target groups may include your peers, friends, parents, teachers, colleagues, pets, the general public, potential love interests and others. While the core of your brand won't change much, you do express and communicate your brand differently to tailor to the target group and what you want it to think of you.

So you may want your teachers to see you as intelligent, interested, open and hard-working, but you will want your peers to see you as cool, trustworthy and maybe a tad rebellious. You will want your parents to see you as filial, responsible and caring, your pets as loving but in-charge and your love interests as sexy, mysterious and rich. In the morning, going to work or school on the train, you may want the general public to see you as sane and normal—unless you belong to a small group who wants to stand out and be seen as different.

Like any brand, you have different tools and channels to communicate these images. This can be through what you say and how you say it, the way you dress, the accessories you use (from rings and piercing, to watches, handphones and laptops), the people you associate with, your body (we all shape our bodies to make them more buff or tall or slim), body language, etc.

A former colleague even went as far as to use different names—one for work and one for clubbing, making it all very confusing indeed.

Brands are similar. They speak to a specific target audience or several audiences and the end goal is to express a specific positioning to these consumers. They want consumers to have a positive image of their brand that is both relevant and differentiated. They try to achieve this by communicating a consistent positioning using a variety of communications media and channels.

To recap, brand positioning is the process of deciding what kind of image you want your target group to have of your brand. When deciding how to position your brand, make sure that whatever positioning you choose is:

YOU ARE A BRAND

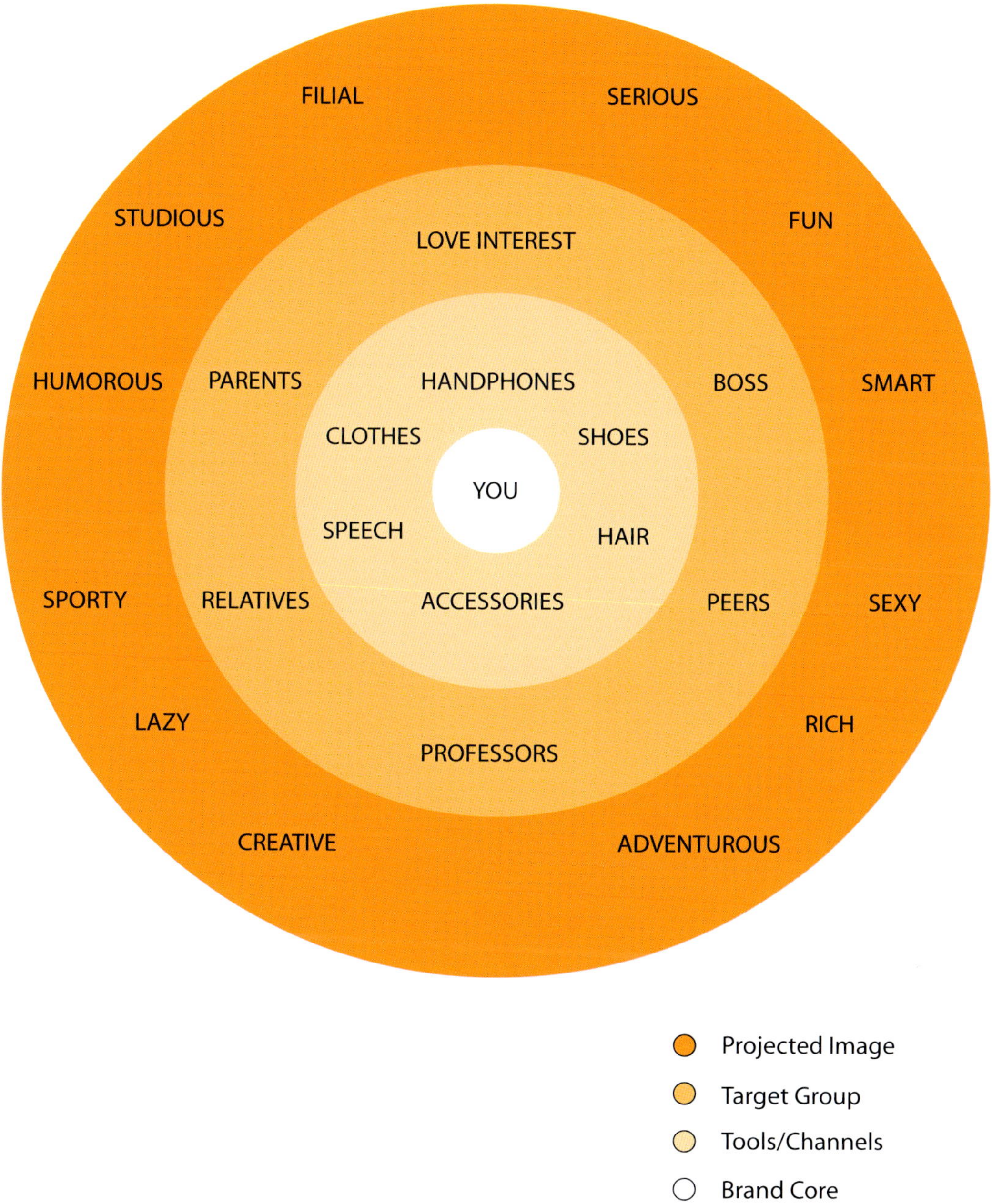

Clear

Nothing is worse than sending confusing messages. The message of "I am this but I am also that" is often used by marketers to reach more than one target group. This won't work. People will just be confused and unsure of what you stand for. Subsequently, they will choose a competitive offer which is more focused.

Differentiated

It is very hard to appeal to consumers and stick in their minds when your positioning adopts an approach that is the same as that of another brand. We call that the "me too" approach. Even if your products or services are the same, you can still find a positioning that will make you stand out. Inflight service between Cathay Pacific, Thai Airways and Singapore Airlines is more or less similar, but Singapore Airlines has managed to own the service by creating the 'Singapore Girl' icon.

If you adopt the same positioning as your competitor, why should consumers choose your brand? With all things being equal, they will decide on price and, before you know it, you will end up caught in a price war that won't benefit anybody. At most, the consumer will benefit for a short time until one of the brands dies, leaving him with less choice and, ultimately, a higher price. So find the 'white space' that you can own.

Relevant

You may find a positioning that is clear and differentiated, but it must also be relevant to your target group. DHL ran a great Ogilvy-campaign that positioned them as the Asian expert ("No one knows Asia like we do"), but research showed that 'local knowledge' is not a factor that ranks highly with the consumer .

Instead, it was a hygiene factor that consumers looked for in all major express companies: Something that needed to be fulfilled before a brand offering the service could even become part of the relevant set.

That's why it's so important to do your homework: A thorough brand audit is crucial because it tells you what your consumers are looking for.

Credible

Consumers in recent years have become increasingly empowered by the Internet. As a result, they have become more critical and often even cynical about brand claims made in advertising. They have been disappointed many a time by irresponsible advertisers, and they have learnt their lesson. As such, they are skeptical of any big claims, especially when they are unsubstantiated by third party support. This is why it's important not to overpromise and to always give the consumer a reason to believe that your claim is true and reassure them that they can trust you with their money.

BRAND EXPRESSION

Once you have determined what you stand for; developed a positioning that is clear, differentiated, relevant and credible; involved your senior management and got them all to sign off on it; you will then need to think about ways of expressing that positioning. Make sure you use all the tools in the box to help people understand what you stand for:

A tagline—a simple line that states what you stand for and what makes you different. FedEx's "We live to deliver" nicely expresses their 'going the extra mile' attitude.

A logo— it could be just your name, or a symbol that expresses your positioning.

A colour—colours can be very useful since they can tap into learnt associations. However, make sure your chosen colour sends the right message in the markets where you operate. Red is auspicious in Asia, but it may be too impactful and is often used as a warning colour in the West.

Imagery—the kind of images you use, the look and feel of your materials, and little details that go all the way down to what's written on your letterheads and brochures reflect your brand's positioning.

So now that you know what you stand for and how to express your positioning, can you go and tell the world? Not so fast. First, think of all the opportunities the consumer has to meet your brand. Not just in your advertising, but how about the shop layout, the staff uniforms, the way the receptionist answers the phones? You need to do some serious:

TOUCHPOINT MANAGEMENT

Touchpoint Management ensures that you send a consistent message about your positioning. That may be hard since it may extend beyond your area of responsibility if you're working in marketing. Unless you're the CEO of the company, you will have to gently invade your colleagues' territories to make sure that, for example, HR plays its role by hiring the right people to live up to the new positioning. Finance must also play its role in the way it reminds customers of late payments, etc. Only if you manage all touchpoints correctly can you give a consistent and convincing message to your potential and existing customers.

Now, can you tell the world? Almost. But before you go and shout it from the mountain top, you have to make sure you're ready internally. You need to spend a moment to think about:

INTERNAL BRANDING

Most of the time, consumers encounter your brand in the shape of your staff. Every single employee is a brand ambassador, whether he has customer contact or not. Even the cleaning lady that tidies up after you have left the office has family and neighbours. They know where she works, and her stories and her attitudes will form her friends' opinion of your company and brand. So you have to empower your staff and make sure they don't just know what your brand stands for but that they are also able to buy into it and live it in their work every day.

The Malaysian Immigration Department provides some good insights. Often its customs officers are the first Malaysians that visitors encounter when they enter the country. First impressions count, and that's why the immigration authority came up with a brand positioning that was both 'friendly and welcoming' for the immigration service. The positioning was to be personified by the customs officers based on an old cliché that read, 'Service with a Smile', complete with printed buttons that their frontline staff wear. But if you land at KLIA, take the train to the other terminal, rush down the escalator and queue up in front of one of the counters and finally find yourself in front of the customs officer, will you get service with a smile? The button may be there, but the smile is often missing. Why? This seems like a typical case of missing Internal Branding. The concept was great and the insight was right, but somewhere down the line, the staff did not buy into it.

BRAND COMMUNICATION

Finally. You have done your homework—research the market and target group. You have decided on a positioning that is clear, differentiated, relevant and credible. You have found the right tagline and look-and-feel that express what you stand for. You have also trained your staff and motivated them to live and breathe your new positioning. Now, you can tell the world.

But can you do it yourself? Sure, you can call a press conference. The CEO can step in front of the microphone and announce your new brand or branding. If you're lucky and there are no major news events that day, you may get a mention in some newspapers and magazines. But after that, nothing. And if you don't have anything new to say, the media won't come to another press conference three months down the line. We have little control over press reports. How they write about you and your positioning may not be what you envisioned. Maybe they misunderstood. Maybe they didn't find it credible and decided to write a skeptical report. Maybe they just didn't care.

That's why you will have to find other ways to communicate what you stand for. You need to find ways that will allow you to stay in charge and control the message, the medium and frequency. You need to harness the power of advertising. But wait—you can't do it alone.

THAM KHAI MENG

Friends of Jörg

Co Chairman,
Executive Regional Creative Director,
Ogilvy & Mather Asia Pacific

Advertising in Asia: What is so unique? What are the highlights, where are they from?

There are 37 countries in Asia, all of them unique. As a result, you have very many distinct types of advertising from Asia. It would be safe to say that Thailand, India, Hong Kong, Japan and Singapore all have their own identifiable brand of advertising.

The Indians are the Latinos of Asia. Their TV spots are usually larger than life with a good measure of exaggerated gesturing and acting thrown in. Perhaps Bollywood, being part of the Indian psyche, has a lot to do with this.

Thailand's slapstick humour is now legendary. It's as if Joe Sedelmaier immigrated there and directed all their commercials.

Hong Kong's TV ads are arty and stylish. That said, there seems to be little substance in most of the ads. The market is tough and, as a result, the industry has become short-term and retail focused. Someone once said, "They used to build brands, but now they brand buildings" referring to the proliferation of real estate advertising. Sadly, their best creatives have migrated to Beijing and Shanghai. That's great news for the Chinese cities but for Hong Kong, there's a hollowing-out of talent.

You'd expect more from the second largest advertising market in the world, but Japan punches way, way below its weight. However, the best work from Japan is weird, wacky and wicked. Nissin Noodles' 'Hungry?' is a great example and remains one of my all-time favourite TV ads. Generally, their TV and online are better than their print.

Conversely, Singapore's specialty is in print. The best ones are intelligent, immaculately crafted and beautifully art-directed; and can take on the best in the world. It takes its influence from British advertising and rewards the audience for their participation. They've become so good at it that they're beating their masters at their own game. Thailand also produces some very good print ads (with the obligatory brand logo for the client in the lower right hand corner).

Will Asian advertising be able to take over the West?

Until China and India eclipse the Western economies, the world will still be dominated by American and European brands. However, even if these countries become the world's leading economies in 10 years' time, it doesn't necessarily mean Asian advertising will be the world's best. Japan has some of the most powerful brands in the world, and the second largest advertising market in the world, and yet the best Honda and Sony TV ads are created in the West, not in Japan. Asian advertisers ironically are publicity-shy. That's the conundrum. The result: Their work doesn't stand out on the global stage.

These days, the world is truly borderless. Although UK and the US still produce a sizeable amount of award-winning work, other countries have now closed the gap. Asian creatives from Thailand, Singapore, Malaysia and, very recently, China have now become a creative force to be reckoned with. According to the Gunn Report, the second most awarded print campaign in 2006 came from China for Nike's 'Run'. I hope that's not a one-off.

Do we still live off creative 'imports' or are we growing our own in Asia? How can we find and nurture talent?

There will always be a place for creative 'imports'. With their diverse experiences and opposing points of view, creative émigrés serve to enrich any local creative community. Outsiders bring with them their own bundle of knowledge and skills set. If you place a barrier for entry to talent, the local community will be the poorer for it. If we seriously want to nurture talent we need to expose them as widely as possible. Protectionism will only stunt the growth of young creatives. Even xenophobic London is opening its doors! The creative director of Fallon London is a young Argentinian.

For this industry to flourish, diversity must be encouraged. Great creative people are pretty nomadic and will cross borders to where they think they can do the best work. As Prof Wasserman once said, "Creative people will go to where creative people are". I couldn't agree more with him.

THAM KHAI MENG

Friends of Jörg

Co Chairman,
Executive Regional Creative Director,
Ogilvy & Mather Asia Pacific

Tham Khai Meng has more than 20 years' advertising experience, working in London, Chicago and across Asia. Today, he is one of the most awarded creatives in the world.

In 1999, Tham joined Ogilvy & Mather and was elected to the Ogilvy & Mather Worldwide Board in 2005.

Under Tham's leadership, the network continues to rise through the regional and global creative rankings—according to *Campaign Brief Asia*, the only regional publication dedicated to profiling Asia's creative product, Tham has been named the No 1 creative director for five consecutive years. And his network has been crowned 'Creative Network of the Year' for the same period.

The year 2006 saw the industry award Ogilvy with the title of 'Network of the Year', the top prize at *Media Magazine*'s 'Agency of the Year' competition. This win was supported by the network's concurrent wins as 'Creative Agency of the Year' and 'One-to-One Agency of the Year'. *Media Magazine*'s 'Agency of the Year' awards have come to represent an invaluable stamp of excellence within the communications industry in Asia.

According to the Gunn Report, the only independent ranking of creative performance globally, Ogilvy & Mather Worldwide is the sixth most creative network in the world. Under Tham's creative leadership, Ogilvy & Mather Asia Pacific contributed a staggering 40% to O&M Worldwide's total score.

In 2005, in recognition of his creative innovation to drive the Ogilvy & Mather Asia Pacific network to its present leadership position, Tham was awarded *Media Magazine*'s hotly contended 'Regional Head of the Year' accolade. This is the first time a creative person has been honoured with this award.

In the same year, Tham made history by becoming the first Asian to chair Clio's executive jury board in the US; he also served as the keynote speaker in Miami at the Clio Awards.

New York-based Advertising Age, a leading global industry commentator, named Tham 'one of the most influential people in the communications business'.

As deputy chairman of the DesignSingapore Council and chairman of its Industry Development Panel, he spearheads the DesignSingapore initiative, positioning Singapore well on its way towards becoming an Asian hub for the creative industry.

Tham holds a BA (1st Class) from Central St. Martin's, UK, and an MA (summa cum laude) in film and history of art from the Royal College of Art, UK. He was recently conferred Fellow of the RCA (FRCA).

Board Memberships

- Board Member: Ogilvy & Mather Worldwide
- Board Member: Urban Redevelopment Authority, Ministry of National Development
- Chairman: Design Industry Panel, Ministry of Information, Communications and the Arts
- Deputy Chairman: Design Council, Ministry of Information, Communications and the Arts
- Teaching Faculty Board (Executive MBA): Steinbeis University Berlin, Germany

CAMPAIGN TITLE
NAVY 'PAGE TURNER' DM

CLIENT
Republic of Singapore Navy

AGENCY
Saatchi & Saatchi Singapore

AGENCY CREDITS

Graham Kelly – Creative Director
Jae Soh, Robin Tan – Art Director
Justine Lee – Copywriter

TIME FRAME OF CAMPAIGN:

2005

CAMPAIGN TITLE

Navy 'Page Turner' DM

OBJECTIVES OF CAMPAIGN

Every year, the Republic of Singapore Navy recruits graduates from the local polytechnics and ITEs—a limited pool of about 5,000. This task is becoming increasingly difficult because of growing demand and competition from other uniformed services (the army, air force, police, etc.) as well as from the private sector.

In 2004, recruitment leads fell by an alarming 30%. Hence, the task for 2005 was to stem the slide and to meet the targets set in the previous year.

TARGET GROUP

The target market for the Navy consists of students aged between 17 and 20. This age group is constantly exposed to many forms of media messaging—all fighting for their attention and seeking to shape changing attitudes and behaviour.

PROPOSITION

Who could resist being the proud 'author' of a captivating autobiography?

COMMUNICATION STRATEGY

The challenge was to create a direct mailer (DM) that would excite the recipients and literally jump at them—engagement was the key. And the most powerful form was to engage people individually.

CHOICE OF MEDIA

Direct Mail

CREATIVE EXECUTION

From this insight, the 'Page Turner' DM was born. A series of highly personalised Navy DMs—designed to look like gripping adventure novels by Tom Clancy and John Grisham—was created. The challenge then was to personalise the DM within the production budget. Thanks to the availability of new printing technology, personalisation was seen in five places in the novel.

And, like actual books, the DMs would have the author's name (each recipient's name) printed on the book cover as well as on the spine. To make it even more engaging, the name and home address were also made part of the copy on the back cover. Inside the book, there was a personalised letter detailing how the recipient could lead an exciting, page-turning life when he joins the Navy. The first reveal inside posed a provocative question: "If your life were a book, would anyone read it?"

A 'life letter', in the form of a bookmark, was included to reinforce the call-to-action. A reply card was placed at the back, just like for mail-order books.

COUNTRIES COVERED

Singapore

RESULTS

The recruitment packs, sent out in May 2005 to polytechnic and ITE graduates, had overwhelming results, far exceeding the client's expectations. Not only did the campaign stem the declining response rate, the 2005 response rate dramatically exceeded the 2004 target by 97%.

What was meant as a Direct Mailer also became a collector's item. Some people even thought that these were actual novels that could be bought at the bookstores!

Introduction

Dear Jimmy Tan,

This is not about writing great autobiographies. It's about living them. And this may very well mark the first chapter of a new and exciting life.

The Republic of Singapore Navy wants to train people like you to become Naval Systems Specialists (NSS). You'll lead a life that has the makings of a great story. And here's why. As a Naval Systems Specialist, you'll:

- Be professionally trained to work on some of the world's most sophisticated technology, at the front line of naval operations.
- Enjoy a challenging job related to your studies.
- Gain a broad range of work experience through job rotation.
- Broaden your horizons by travelling overseas to interesting places.
- Work in unique environments, like naval bases, warships, and on our latest frigates, submarines and maritime patrol aircraft.

As well, you'll enjoy advantages you may not find in the private sector. For example, you can:

- Receive a lump sum of up to $19,680 under the Joint Poly-SAF Diploma Scheme (JPSDS). Or $15,000 under the Diploma Induction Scheme (DIS).
- Get a starting salary of $1,985, increasing to $2,065 after just 3 months.
- Receive monthly shipboard allowance of $200-$300, or submarine allowance of $700, plus overseas allowances.
- Get a lump sum of 10 months' salary upon completion of service.

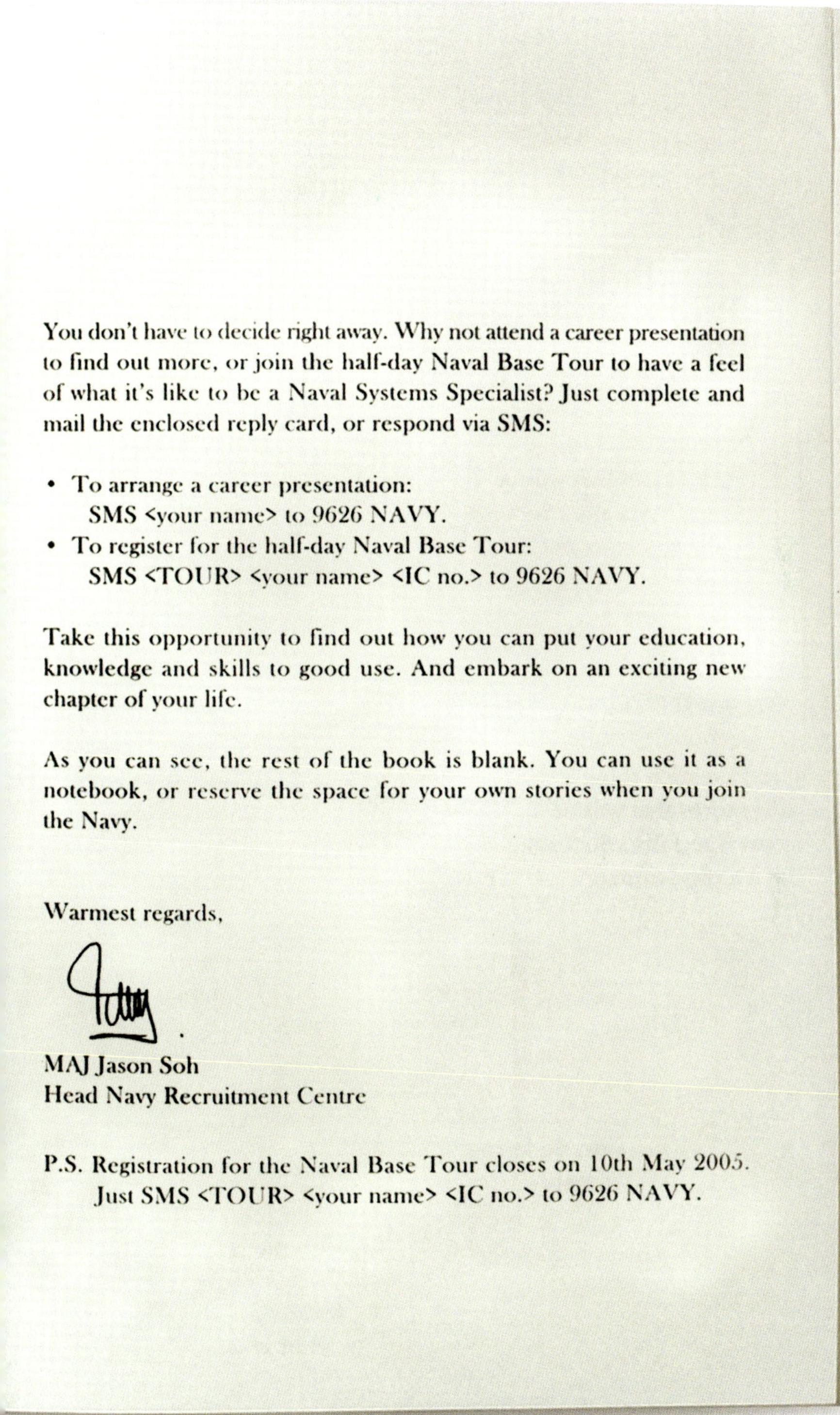

You don't have to decide right away. Why not attend a career presentation to find out more, or join the half-day Naval Base Tour to have a feel of what it's like to be a Naval Systems Specialist? Just complete and mail the enclosed reply card, or respond via SMS:

- To arrange a career presentation:
  SMS <your name> to 9626 NAVY.
- To register for the half-day Naval Base Tour:
  SMS <TOUR> <your name> <IC no.> to 9626 NAVY.

Take this opportunity to find out how you can put your education, knowledge and skills to good use. And embark on an exciting new chapter of your life.

As you can see, the rest of the book is blank. You can use it as a notebook, or reserve the space for your own stories when you join the Navy.

Warmest regards,

MAJ Jason Soh
Head Navy Recruitment Centre

P.S. Registration for the Naval Base Tour closes on 10th May 2005.
Just SMS <TOUR> <your name> <IC no.> to 9626 NAVY.

Prologue

The Indian Ocean. Latitude: 08° 38' N. Longitude: 75° 15' E. 0428 hrs. The Combat Information Centre falls silent as the Chief Action Information Systems Operator calmly reports: "Skunk 103, bearing 215 range 45, tracking 120-15, now classified HOSTILE!" "Roger. Plan missile 1 on Hostile 103," orders the Principal Warfare Officer.

"Missile ready". A few heart-pounding seconds later, his command rings out: "Engage missile 1!" Without hesitation, you fire the Harpoon missile at Mach 1.

You feel the adrenaline surge through your body. Tension mounts as the deadly weapon streaks towards its target at 1 metre above sea level. The atmosphere is electric... everyone in the Combat Information Centre silently watches the countdown... 5 seconds, 4, 3, 2, 1, impact! Then a wave of elation... "Hostile 103 destroyed!" This was just an exercise. Next time it could be for real...

There's no such thing as a typical day in the Navy. These are the sort of adventures that will be a part of your life when you become a Naval Systems Specialist. So keep the rest of the book for your journals. And make it a page-turner.

HALF-DAY NAVAL BASE TOUR
Be a Naval Systems Specialist for a day. Get your hands on sophisticated weapons. Board state-of-the-art naval vessels. And get a behind-the-scenes look at the naval base. Other than fun and excitement, refreshments will also be provided. Just send us your particulars before 10th May 2005, and we'll contact you with details on the visit.
To register: Complete and mail the enclosed reply card. Or SMS: <TOUR> <your name> <IC no.> to 9626 NAVY.

LEE JIN WEN
UNCHARTED DEPTHS
A true story
SOH ENG KIAT
STEALTH FORCE
A true story

LEE JIN WEN
SOH ENG KIAT
is a young Singaporean who
embarked on an extraordinary life in 2005.
Opening in the author's home at
14 Upper Bukit Timah View
Singapore 588144
this book serves as an autobiography
of the writer's experiences as a Naval Systems Specialist.
Operating, controlling and maintaining
state-of-the-art warships and weaponry.
Duties that take the writer around the world.
It's a life full of excitement, challenges,
and discoveries. A must-read for those
who aspire to live life to the fullest.
"A no-holds-barred,
pull-out-all-the-stops thriller."

JIMMY TAN
is a young Singaporean who
embarked on an extraordinary life in 2005
Opening in the author's home at
5B Ridley Park, #05-01
Tanglin Park
Singapore 248478
SINGAPORE
PP 02177
William Tan
Blk 5 Tampines Avenue 5 #08-58
Singapore 5805

If your life was a book,
would anyone read it?

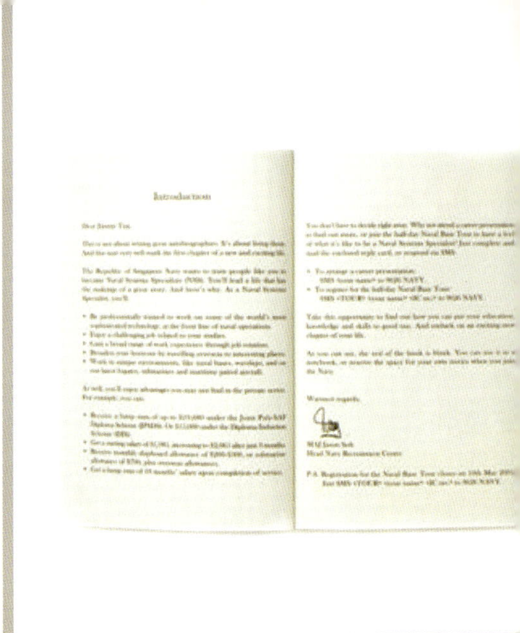
Introduction

Prologue
HALF-DAY NAVAL BASE TOUR

REPLY CARD

LEE JIN WEN
UNCHARTED DEPTHS
A true story
SOH ENG KIAT
STEALTH FORCE
A true story

"A no-holds-barred, pull-out-all-the-stops thriller."

SINGAPORE
William Tan
Blk 5 Tampines Avenue 5 #08-58
Singapore 5805

The page-turner DM not only proved highly effective in generating recruitment leads, it also generated considerable attention at the following creative award competitions:

Award 2005, Australia
Bronze (Direct Mail)

Campaign Brief "The Work—2005", Australia
Direct Mail

DM Asia 2005
Finalist (Best Craft in Copywriting)
Finalist (Best Craft in Art Direction)

The Singapore Creative Circle Awards 2005
Finalist (Design Direct Mail)

Institute of Advertising, Singapore Hall of Fame Awards 2005
Grand Winner (Relationship Marketing Campaign of the Year)

YoungGuns International Advertising Award
Silver (Direct Mail)

John Caples International Awards
First Place, Best of Show (Consumer Single Non-Profit Direct Mail Dimensional)

Asia Pacific Advertising Awards (AdFest 2006)
Silver (Direct Marketing, Dimensional Mail)

2. The ad agency

The Hall of Fame

Advertising History, as with all history, is often shaped by a few individuals who changed the way we do and look at things. Any selection is naturally subjective, but here are three names everybody in advertising must know:

Bill Bernbach

Bernbach is often credited as the father of modern advertising. Claim to fame: Teaming up copywriters and art directors. His new agency, Doyle Dane Bernbach (DDB), created the memorable Volkswagen Beetle campaign ('Snowplough', 'Think Small', and 'Lemon') in the 60s. Today, DDB is one of the world's leading advertising networks that is highly respected for its creativity.

David Ogilvy

In a way, Ogilvy is Bernbach's UK equivalent. He was the founder of Ogilvy & Mather and has since authored numerous publications to explain how advertising works. Claim to fame: The Rolls Royce print ad. Today, O&M is yet another one of the world's leading advertising networks, particularly in the Asian market.

Leo Burnett

Burnett is better known as the creator of The Marlboro Man or Tony the Tiger. After all, these are famous icons, conceived by Burnett himself, who was a trained journalist. A hall-of-fame copywriter, Burnett was one of the first ad men to understand branding and what it means to build a name upon an image. He is best remembered for these Burnett icons: a pencil, the red apples on every desk at the reception area and for his agency slogan, 'Reaching for the stars'.

At this stage, let's have a look at the different departments within an agency and see what their functions and roles are:

ACCOUNT MANAGEMENT

Sometimes called 'Client Services'. Or 'Account Service'. Management is the better—and more appropriate—term since this describes more accurately what account managers do. They don't serve the client; they manage the overall account—from first taking the client brief to making sure the internal processes run smoothly, looking after timings and costs, and ensuring the overall profitability of the account for the agency. Account managers know the clients' business inside out and have the clients' best (business) interests at heart. They are the gatekeepers of each advertising project, and most importantly, they handle the relationship with the client.

Client management is all about relationships: Clients need to feel that the agency cares about them personally and about their brand. Clients need attention and, sometimes, pampering. Clients need to feel important and occasionally need a listening ear. Many of the best ad campaigns have been based on great client-agency relationships, and great account managers have often been invited to make a switch to join the client team. The strength of a client-agency relationship can make or break the account. If the relationship is good and the client trusts the agency, he is prepared to overlook small mistakes. If the relationship is bad, a minor mistake can lead to the agency losing a multi-million dollar account.

So How Do You Build A Good Client Relationship?

As an Account Management staff you should:

- know as much as you can about the client's business. Be eager to learn. Read up in your spare time.
- show the client that you care. Go the extra mile and prove that this account is not just a job for you. Demonstrate that you love the brand as much as the client loves it.
- always be honest and open. If the client has overpaid you, return the money. If a mistake is made, be the first to tell it to the client as well as inform him how you will remedy it. Don't hide the error and assume your client won't find out. He will.
- be respectful, even when there is nobody listening. Walls have ears. Yes, the work can be sometimes frustrating and, once in a while, a client's decision may seem incomprehensible to you since there is no way of understanding the pressures and restrictions he has. Even so, it's never a 'stupid client'. Try to see his reasons. Even if you still don't agree, ultimately, he is the client.
- be outspoken. The client has hired you not to hear that everything he does is perfect. He knows it isn't. He needs your expertise and input, so have an opinion and don't be afraid to express it with the necessary support. Be open enough to listen to the other side but do speak up.

Some agencies have an additional level, that of Account Supervisor, which can be relatively senior or junior, depending on the agency. Most agency heads in the big networks were once from account management since their positions require the skills they have picked up in their account management career—managing the client and, over time, taking up more and more personnel responsibility within the agency.

STRATEGIC PLANNING

Also known as 'Account Planning'. This deals with looking at the big picture—global industry trends and consumer research. It's about being able to read statistics and interpreting what they mean for a product or service. It's about searching for the one consumer insight that can be the basis of a creative idea or concept. With Johnnie Walker, for example, the insight was: Every man wants to advance. The advertising idea was: Keep Walking.

Strategic planning used to be part of account management, but the world became too complex and the daily nitty-gritty too encompassing, and thus was planning born as a separate department. Some say this change first started at BMP in London.

Planners have it easy with the client—they can talk about the brand core, the big picture and industry movements. They don't have to argue about timing and cost. However, they need to be able to talk to creative teams and to develop a single-minded proposition that is truly single-minded and not multiple choice. Planning found its way into most agencies in Europe and the US, and it's becoming more and more common in Asia.

It is possible for senior staff in account management to cross over to strategic planning. It is more difficult for planners to cross over to account management unless they are willing to start at the bottom of the ladder. This is due largely to the fact that account management skills can only be picked up gradually over time. Someone who joins the account management staff in a senior position without having acquired his skills along the way will experience many knowledge gaps. This may make it difficult for him to be accepted and respected by junior staff who know more.

CREATIVE DEPARTMENT

The creatives are the ideas people. How do they do it? There is no magic formula. Different creatives have different ways to get inspired. All are very much in touch with the world or their part of the world. They are passionate about film, art, fashion, comics, alternative culture, music and/or design. They get inspired by watching films, listening to songs or simply sitting in a café and observing people.

They are free spirits and they hate formality. Account managers, who are commonly attired in corporate wear, are called 'suits' by the creatives, who prefer to express their own brand through their long hair, beard and comfortable clothes. Creatives hate generalisations and stereotypes and have a tendency to fall in love with their ideas but are also willing to fight for them. A concise brief helps them to focus their thoughts but sometimes their passion takes them to the extreme. When this happens, they may even forget the brand and the initial brief.

They love recognition by their peers in award shows. The Cannes Lions International Advertising Festival is their church, the Gold Lion their idol. They look down on all non-creatives. And they smoke. Many of them smoke. I guess it helps them think.

How Do Creatives Work?

Since Bill Bernbach's time, creatives have worked in teams comprising:

- Copywriters who write the text in the ad—headline and body copy—and often come up with the creative concept, and
- Art Directors who find the right picture, typeface, colour and composition for the ad.

These may start as junior copywriters or art directors and, if they prove themselves, will move up to become senior copywriters or art directors. The next rung up is the Creative Director (CD) who is in charge of, and leads, several teams. The CD who oversees the overall creative output of the agency is often called the Executive Creative Director (ECD). In many creative agencies, the ECD runs the agency in tandem with the CEO.

The sequence of promotions can be curious—a good creative mind may be promoted all the way up the chain to Creative Director, forgetting that this position requires a different skills set. Because many creatives work in teams of two and spend their time thinking up campaign ideas, often with no training in people management, they may find themselves not cut out for this responsibility. All of a sudden, in their new role, they find themselves without a partner but are still required to develop ideas, evaluate the teams' ideas and motivate and encourage the creative teams at the same time. Some Creative Directors have turned out to be great creatives but famously bad directors, tearing up ideas they find unsuitable and throwing tantrums.

ADMINISTRATION

This department undertakes the following responsibilities: Finance and HR which are often, unfortunately, managed by the same person, presenting him with the dilemma of two conflicting roles—motivating staff, often through a pay rise, on the one hand and controlling overall cost on the other; Accounting (accounts, not account management); Secretaries and Traffic, whose job it is to support account management by making sure that the workflow is smooth for every job and that all the relevant sign-offs are obtained, especially for the finished artwork.

STUDIO / PRODUCTION

This department used to paste up artwork by hand, but with computerisation, layouts are now accomplished through DTP or desktop publishing. Studio and Production now produce films or digital files for printing and help to check the colour on colour proofs. Production also makes sure the right photographer or director is engaged and that timing and costs are adhered to.

Everybody in the agency line-up is involved in developing the next big advertising campaign. And they can only work well if they are given a clear brief.

ANDREW LOK

Friends of Jörg

Greater China Creative Director,
Ogilvy & Mather Asia Pacific

"And this too shall pass"

From now on, if I'm eating meat in China, I'll try to make sure I can see it. I watched a report on Beijing TV about how cardboard boxes are recycled by soaking them in caustic soda until pulp is formed, and then this mush is mixed with fatty pork and stuffed into steamed buns.

Every moment I spend here, I come across new horrors like that. I love it.

Pore through the news and you'll find hundreds of stories each day relating to the chaos and lack of civil society in China, but they are merely the birth pangs of what could be the most interesting experiment of the 21st century. Put simply, after a long tryst with socialism, 1.3 billion Chinese are being allowed to do what Chinese do best: Make money.

And they are making it by the bucket loads. In the two decades since Deng Xiao Ping declared it was okay for some in China to "get rich first", private enterprise and foreign investment here has lifted more people out of poverty than at any other time in human history.

Sure, the enormous disparity between the 'haves' and 'have-nots' is deplorable, but rewind to the early days of two great modern nations, Great Britain and the United States, and you find parallels. Friedrich Engels' description of Manchester during the Industrial Revolution:

"Such is the Old Town of Manchester, and, on re-reading my description, I am forced to admit that instead of being exaggerated, it is far from black enough to convey a true impression of the filth, ruin, and uninhabitableness, the defiance of all considerations of cleanliness, ventilation, and health... And such a district exists in the heart of the second city of England, the first manufacturing city of the world. If any one wishes to see in how little space a human being can move, how little air—and such air!—he can breathe, how little of civilisation he may share and yet live, it is only necessary to travel hither." But consider this Mr Engels: On the backs of these cotton workers, and with a little help from the cannon of her navy, Britain built her empire.

Likewise, as a depiction of the immigrant slums in 1860s Manhattan, Scorsese's violent *Gangs of New York* is far from historically accurate, but as historian Tyler Anbinder affirms, "When the Irish first came to America... they literally did have to fight for their fair share of what America had to offer."

And while it's true America then was already on its way to becoming a powerful nation, the flood of hardworking immigrants in the late 19th century, doing whatever it takes to survive and prosper, accelerated the setting of the stage for America's ascendancy to superpower status in the 20th century.

China today echoes these examples.

Barring the occasional reprehensible case of slavery (as I'm writing this, an Internet news alert tells me that "a Chinese court today sentenced a man to death and jailed another 28 people for their roles in a slave labour scandal at brick factories in the northern province of Shanxi"), local and multinational factories in China—that manufacture most of the things we use in our daily lives—are responsible for creating thousands of jobs daily for an exponentially expanding population and for making the China an economic force to be reckoned with. To paraphrase Jeffrey Sachs, the factory is the first stage of a country's climb up the ladder of development. It ain't pretty, but it works.

On a similar note, when you take a close look at the vast contrast between the gleaming towers of cities like Shanghai and the poverty amongst China's rural denizens (about 80% of total population), you might start to wonder if the 'China Miracle' is largely still hype. But one only has to see the ambition and hunger in the eyes of the tens of thousands of people arriving daily into cities like Beijing, Shanghai and Guangzhou from the inefficient farms and closed-down state enterprises of different Chinese provinces to know that they are a people eager to better their lives and prove their mettle by any means necessary.

Therefore, while drastic social inequalities and grave lapses in ethics are prevalent everywhere today in China, they are issues that will only be resolved in time after a critical mass in society acquires the middle-class material base it needs from which to comfortably assess what the dominant values are that makes them, them.

So how can a brand stand out positively amongst all this flux?

1. Be clear about what you stand for. In the ethical vacuum of a Chinese society primarily concerned with material acquisition at all costs, more and more consumers are hungry for a coherent set of values. Most find it in a mixture of rediscovering Chinese culture and embracing imported Western liberalism. Where is your brand's stake in this virgin ground?

2. Be accountable. Chinese consumers are hungry for what you have to say. It's all news to them. But the moment you don't walk the walk, they'll abandon you, without a thought, for one of the plethora of other brands, local and foreign, clamouring for their attention.

3. Be mindful of your power. Believe it or not, in China, you can actually change the world. The brands a Chinese consumer champions will have a rippling effect across the globe because of the sheer scale of this market. Will these brands be made and marketed with socially desirable values, e.g. "green consciousness"? Do these brands encourage a trust-driven business environment by advocating product quality and integrity, and then following through on these promises? Will these brands embrace causes that rally communities, or set examples of how a modern society can balance the satisfaction of individual wants with the establishment of a common good within a rules-based system?

To end serendipitously, and with perfect irony, just before wrapping up this article in an airport lounge, I took a break and picked up a 19th July issue of *China Daily*. Here's what I read. "A TV report… that showed… softened chopped cardboard as the main ingredient in steamed buns has been dismissed as false news… investigations had found an employee… fabricated the sensational program for higher audience ratings." He's just another Chinese person doing whatever it takes to get ahead. And perhaps the fact he got caught crossing the line is just one of many small incremental signs that things are getting better. I am an eternal optimist. Steamed buns anybody?

ANDREW LOK

Greater China Creative Director, Ogilvy & Mather Asia Pacific

Andrew Lok started his career in Singapore as a journalist with United Press International. After he decided it was more interesting to create news than to report it, he joined the advertising industry. His first agency was Bozell, followed by DDB, Batey, Y&R and TBWA.

Then he left for China, where he won the nationwide BMW account. He helped in setting up the Interone BBDO office in Beijing to service this business, after which he headed back south to helm O & M Guangzhou.

In 12 months, he raised that agency's creative ranking in China from nowhere to No 8. Following that, he was shipped back home to lead David Communications Singapore, an Ogilvy boutique. In a repeat performance, he raised that agency's creative ranking in Singapore from nowhere to No 18 in one year.

His work has been featured in One Show, Clio, Cannes, and, most importantly to him, his mother's scrapbook.

Currently, he is based in Beijing as Creative Director of Ogilvy Greater China.

He is still trying to figure out the chord progressions and substitutions required to play jazz guitar. Among the many nicknames given to him by industry peers, some of which are not suitable to be published, his favourite is "The Locksmith".

AN ADVERTISING AGENCY

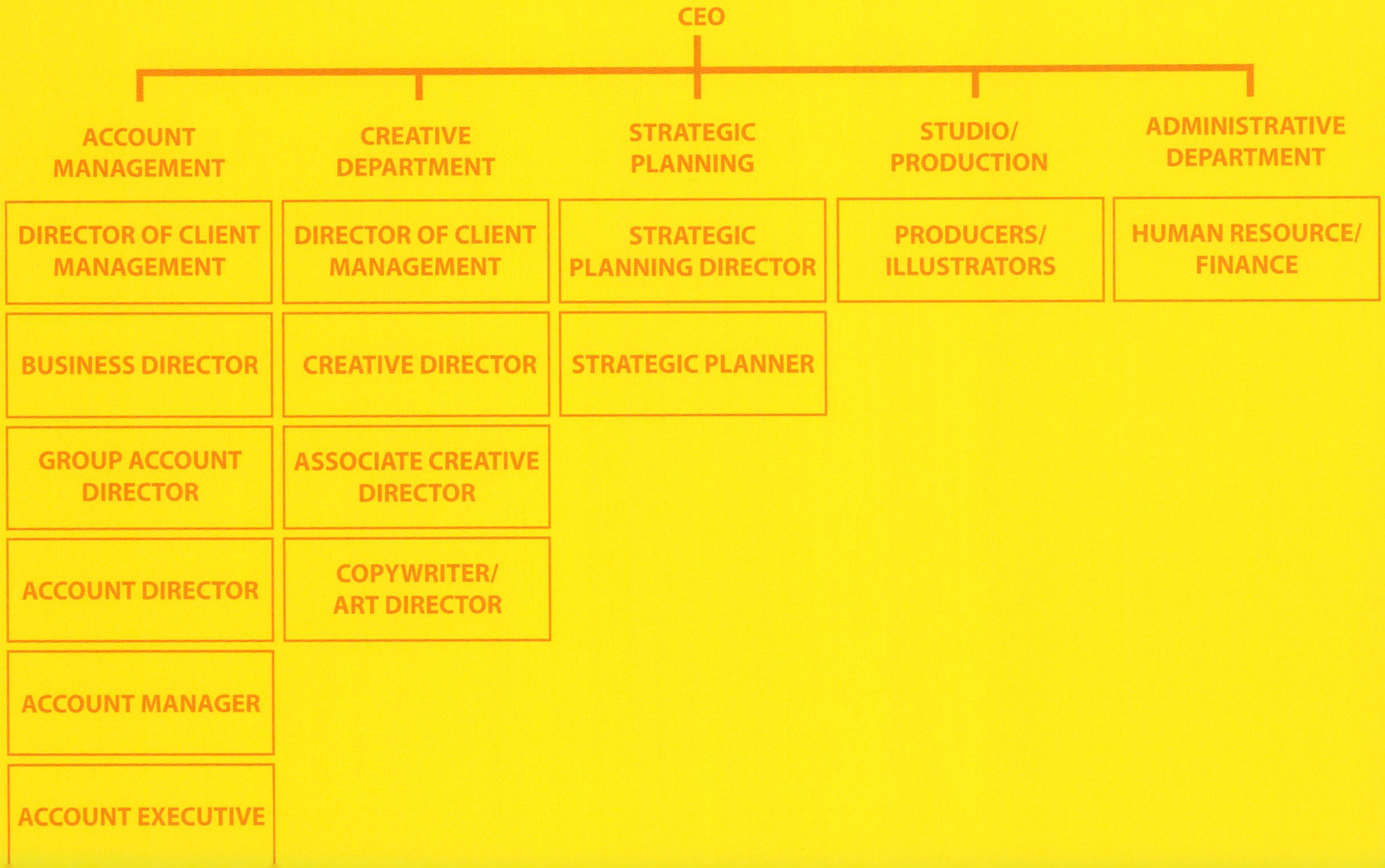

Yesterday we received the brief for the first Happy Jelly campaign. Gosh! They want everything! Talk to children AND parents! Talk about colours AND tastes! What happened to Happiness? Wow, I am glad I am not the account director!

CAMPAIGN TITLE
VERTICAL FOOTBALL
CLIENT
adidas
AGENCY
TBWA/Japan.

AGENCY CREDITS

John Merrifield – Creative Director
Hirofumi Nakajima – Art Director
John Merrifield – Copywriter
Akinori Otani – Facilitator

TIME FRAME OF CAMPAIGN

September 2003

CAMPAIGN TITLE

Vertical Football

OBJECTIVES OF CAMPAIGN

Add fuel to the launch of a global football campaign while facing the most cluttered outdoor market on the planet.

TARGET GROUP

Japanese youth

PROPOSITION

Own the passion and you own the game.

COMMUNICATION STRATEGY

Turn the oldest medium in the world into the most innovative. Take the 'beautiful game' to death-defying heights. Turn advertising into entertainment.

CHOICE OF MEDIA

2 large billboards overlooking the most crowded pedestrian intersections in Tokyo and Osaka.

CREATIVE EXECUTION

1. Media Strategy

Turn the oldest medium in the world into the most innovative. Due to its omnipresence, outdoor advertising here is largely invisible. We needed to come up with something that would literally stop people in their tracks. (Humans had never been attached to billboards here before.) Creating the world's first vertical pitch on billboards peering down upon the trendy retail areas of Shibuya (Tokyo) and Dotonbori (Osaka) succeeded far beyond expectations.

2. Creative Executions in Each Individual Media

All billboards are vertical. All football pitches are horizontal. Our first idea was a horizontal billboard. It would jut out from a building about 5 storeys up, a sort of mini 'pitch' complete with goalposts. Four players would get into a bit of 2 on 2 in full view of the crowds below. The client loved it. Then we got the quote. Shit. Um, er … all right how about this: What if we cheat physics and have a vertical pitch with players and ball hanging from ropes. And we'll get that big billboard that's ten storeys up on top of the building overlooking Hachiko, the world's busiest pedestrian intersection. And that's precisely what we did. Isn't it wonderful that Japan's so damn expensive?

For the first time in history, the beautiful game was taken to death-defying heights, with two players and a ball suspended from ropes ten storeys above the ground and at a 90-degree angle to the 'pitch'.

3. Integrated / Harmonised Effort

The signature visual element of the global campaign was the vivid green of a football pitch. This not only worked well on television and in print, but enabled us to get very innovative with the world's oldest medium: Outdoor. The campaign theme, "Own the game", was also further strengthened by the headline on the billboard pitch: "Own the passion and you own the game".

4. Value for Money

Not only did it receive the most publicity of any advertisment in Japan in 2003, it made the front cover of the *Wall Street Journal* (globally) as well as in major news, sports and entertainment broadcasts in more than 90 countries around the world, earning over US$160 million dollars in free publicity.

adidas
> 情熱を制す者が、ゲームを制す。

adidas

者が、ゲーム

和真メガネ

COUNTRIES COVERED

Japan

RESULTS

Over US$160 million in free publicity worldwide to date.

Cannes	2 Gold Lions 1 Media Gold Lion
Clios	Grand Clio 2 Gold Clios
One Show	2 Gold Pencils
D&AD	Acceptance in Book
Communication Arts	Acceptance in Book
AWARD	1 Gold Pencil
YoungGuns	1 Gold Bullet
Ad Fest	Best of the Best (Outdoor) 1 Gold Lotus
Asian Advertising Awards	1 Gold Spike (Best of Outdoor) 2 Silver Spikes
Japan ADC Awards	ADC Prize (equivalent of gold)
The Work Book	Appearance in Book
Gunn Report	Third most awarded print work of 2004

3. The process

Client Brief. It is essential that the client briefs the agency thoroughly and in writing. The better and more thorough the brief, the better the final campaign can work. Here is a sample template to provide a framework about what the agency should know and questions that the clients should ask themselves before embarking on a project:

Agency Brief

Client (name and address):

Project Name:

Date:

Tentative Launch Date:

Background Information

History of product:
Key challenge:
Target audience:
Advertising goal:
Key message:
Support:
Creative consideration:

Timeline

Agency briefing date:
Creative presentation date:
Campaign launch date:

It is common sense that the client should brief the agency in writing—this way, both sides have a document to refer to and arguments can easily be resolved. However, often in our busy lives, clients will brief the agency verbally, either on the phone or in person. To remedy the situation, the agency should write down the brief in a client brief format, re-present it to the client and ask: "Just to make sure, is this what you want us to do?"

At the same time, the ad agency should be briefed to look out for the best ways to reach the target and to look for some interesting channels to get the message across. A media brief could look like this:

Media Brief

Client (name and address) :
Project Name:
Presentation Date:

Background Information

- What is the business environment?
- What are the key business seasons?
- Who are the major competitors?
- What is the client's brand awareness and perception performance?
- What are the business goals? Any specific focus of the business?
- What brand positioning do we want?

Target Audience

- Whom are we talking to? Demographic and Psychographic?
- Any worthy specific consumer response to share? Complaints / Appreciation?

Role of Advertising

- What company objectives do we want the advertising to achieve? (General awareness? To induce action? To change perception? For acquisition?)
- Are there any other communication channels required?

Market Coverage

- How many markets are we covering?
- What is the priority within these markets?

Creative Unit

- What are the creative works available? Television commercial (TVC)? Print? Others?
- Is colour required? 4-colour (4c)? Or black-and-white (b/w)?
- What is the duration of the TVC?
- For print, what is the size and format? Horizontal? Vertical? Banner? Half-page (HP)? Full-page (FP)?
- How many versions are there?

Budget

- What is the planned media budget? (Please state clearly whether it is tax inclusive.)

An important part of these briefs is the budget. As a client, you need to be fair to the agency and give them a budget, even in a pitch. Don't tell them, "I don't have a budget; tell me how much I should spend" because that's not true. Of course you have a budget. Not giving the agency a figure will only lead to frustration on both sides. With no limitations, the agency will more often than not propose ideas that are beyond your actual budget. At the end of the day, you will find that you won't be able to afford an idea that you may love.

So how do you determine, if you are the head of marketing, how large a budget you should have? Most of the time, you won't have a choice. Your budget is given to you, top down, by your CEO. He knows the overall situation of the company and is familiar with expenses such as staff costs, rent, investment, appreciation, interest, sales incentives, marketing, etc. He will divide up the overall cake and give you your piece. It's then your job to make the most of it. Is this the best way to determine the marketing budget? Maybe not, but that's how it works most of the time.

What would be a better way? Naturally, it's 'bottom up'. You start by setting objectives for the company. What is it trying to achieve in the coming financial year, and how can advertising and marketing contribute? Maybe you want to increase sales. Advertising can help by increasing awareness and top-of-mind recall. Sales can then make sure the distribution is efficient, and together you can do some on-premise promotions to stimulate trial. If your product is great and the price is right, your sales could increase.

Once you have established your objectives, you explore the measures necessary to reach those objectives. Do you need a big TV campaign to reach your target? If so, how many waves are needed during one year and what should the frequency of exposure be? Are your objectives more accessible through the Internet? Should you concentrate on sales promotions instead and budget for heavy sampling?

The choice of measures determines your cost. If everybody agrees on the objectives, it's up to you as the expert to decide on the measures needed to meet your objectives. Once the measures have been agreed on, they will come at a price, which determines your budget for the year.

In many cases, you will not have the ideal scenario of being given the funds that you need to achieve all the objectives. You may need to prioritise or discuss with your agency how to find more effective and efficient ways to reach your target. Great, simple and very creative solutions can often make up for a missing media budget and still work so much better and be more impactful and memorable than the conventional.

Enlightened CEOs may have a number in mind, but they will still ask all departments to come up with a budget based on an ideal world-scenario. In a management meeting, every department head will have the opportunity to present his budget and argue for it. The end result will usually be an allocated budget which is not ideal but which every department can live and work with.

STRATEGIC PLANNING

The strategic planner takes the client brief and translates it into something the creative teams can use. Much of the information given in the client brief is important for the planner and account manager, but too much for the creative. So the planner develops the creative brief using a few tools at his disposal:

Market Research

As mentioned before, it is vital that you know your target group and what motivates and moves them. Different people have different needs and may be at different stages of development.

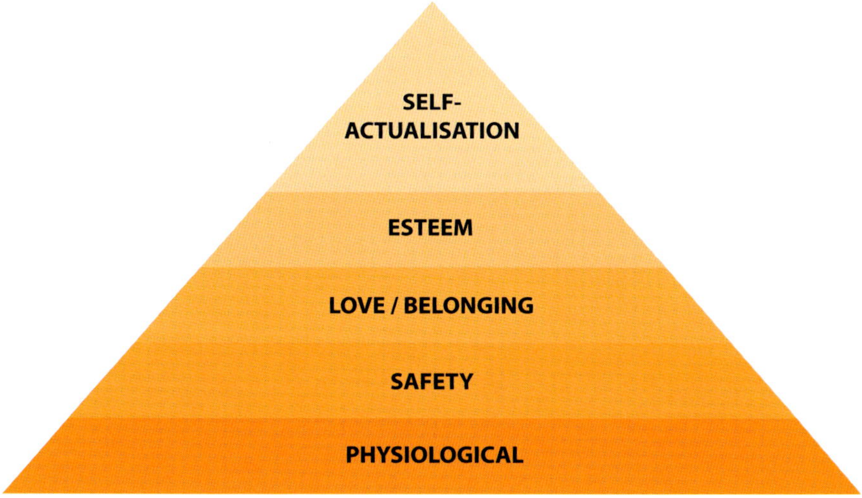

MASLOW'S HIERARCHY OF NEEDS

Everybody in advertising, branding and communications should know Maslow's pyramid of needs and what level—or levels—the needs of his target are on. This can help determine the advertising message and its delivery; tapping into a specific need renders the target group more open to the advertising message.

For example, an advertisement for a fabric softener may tap into a mother's need for love and social acceptance. It appeals to the target on the promise that she will be seen as a 'good mother' if she uses the product. In the same way, an advertisement for a car or expensive watch may tap into their target's esteem needs by positioning their product as a status symbol and communicating what it says about the owner; similarly, an advertisement for a lingerie brand may tap into the self-actualisation needs of their target and use a line like "When only you know."

There are many ways to find out what consumers think and how they behave. Proctor and Gamble placed cameras in people's homes a few years ago in Thailand, but other less invasive means include anything from online questionnaires to feedback-forms and focus groups.

The use of focus groups as a research method is popular and a good tool to gauge consumer sentiment when done right. With a good moderator and discussion flow, focus groups can uncover consumers' attitudes towards brands and suss out their purchase motivations and barriers.

Sometimes, focus groups are used to test advertising concepts or finished advertisements especially in situations where clients are hesitant if a concept would be understood and accepted by their target (after all, the focus group can be used as a reason if the campaign flops as there is always the excuse: "But the focus group liked it!").

For ad testing, there are two major limitations that one should be aware of:

Expectations. The group is in an artificial environment. People leave their homes and offices and come together to sit in a room with strangers and discuss a product. In their minds, they may wonder why they have been invited and what the expectations are. That may cause them to be more critical than they would usually be. After all, being too positive may be misunderstood as being 'dumb' by the other group members. Also, people evaluate ideas and concepts by referencing other executions they have previously seen. That may lead to very new or original concepts being rejected, since there is no prior experience to reference.

Format. For cost reasons, it makes sense to test a concept or TV storyboard before the ad is produced and costs are incurred. The problem is that this requires a change of format. Instead of a finished print ad, the group discusses a layout. Instead of a finished TV commercial with the right music, sounds and talent, the group looks at the storyboard, which comprises drawings of scenes or the same pictures filmed with some motion added (an animatic) or scenes from films and other commercials cut together (a stealomatic). The discussion then happens on a very rational level, leaving out the emotional connection that visual media often establishes.

Consumer Behaviour—How Consumers Learn And Make Decisions

Research would look beyond Maslow. Most planners have a good understanding of consumer behaviour and they look at how consumers learn communication messages and also what drives them to make the purchases that they make. For example, would they buy a car more to impress their neighbours or for its design, comfort and performance? Such purchasing choices, which are made solely in the interest of image, are a common problem for understated brands.

These learnings would find their way into the Creative Brief that will help to determine the most effective use of communication strategies. These include the use of a symbol, known in technical terms as semiotics and seen in 'The Marlboro Man'; classical conditioning, as tested out with Pawlow's dog experiment where existing stimuli are used to position the products or service; and humour, because we remember better when we laugh.

Another point to consider in consumer behaviour is focus. A creative director (CD) I know used to throw a tennis ball at his client in the middle of a presentation. The client always caught the ball. After some time, the CD would suddenly throw five tennis balls, overwhelming the client who would not be able to catch a single one. What this illustrated was that you really have to concentrate on just the one message that you want to communicate. This is the single-minded proposition; if done right, the message will stick. At the end of the day, if you try to send out too many messages at the same time, no one will remember any of them. It's a hard lesson to learn for clients who have so much to say about their service or product.

Eventually, when the research is complete, the findings are translated from the client brief into a :

CREATIVE BRIEF

The creative teams sit down with the planner and account management to be briefed. They are never just given the written brief without the opportunity to ask questions. During this meeting, planners and account management staff explain more of the background to the brief, the point of certain deliverables and restrictions that the creatives must work with. Creatives will also ask questions and make sure they have really understood what the client wants and to minimise the possibility of the client rejecting their work.

After this briefing, the creatives begin their work. Far from taking place in a vacuum, the creative process involves plenty of referencing to popular culture, books and art. The creatives observe their surroundings wherever they are and use their observations in their scripts and layouts. They look at other ads and get inspired to develop an idea further or sometimes, to copy it.

They then discuss their different ideas and thoughts with their CD and then present them in an initial internal meeting within the agency. During this meeting, planning and account management give feedback as to which directions are the most promising. The creative teams go back and develop the selected directions further and present their ideas again, this time with layout and script. Two or three alternatives are chosen for client presentation, and these get developed even further. Layouts become ads, scripts are turned into storyboards, and these are then presented to the client.

Who presents the work to the client? There is no rule. It very much depends on who can present the ideas best. Some creatives are very good at presenting their work; they have a picture in their mind of how the presentation should sound and feel like, and they manage to get this picture across effectively. One example is Michael Hart, formerly Creative Director at DDB Hong Kong, who is one of the best presenters I have ever met. Then, there are some creatives who may be extremely talented and full of great ideas, but who are terrible at presenting their work. They get flustered, start stammering, turn red and are unable to get the intended message across. In such cases, it's always better to get the account manager to do the job.

Creative Brief

Client:
Product:
Date:

Brand Idea:

Brand Personality:

- What are we trying to accomplish for the brand long-term?
- What are we trying to accomplish in this ad? (Advertising objective)
- Whom are we talking to? (Consumer insights that will make our message relevant)
- What is it that we want to communicate and how do we think it will work?
- What exactly do we want the audience to think and do? (Desired impact)
- The proposition that will trigger change

Supporting reasons that can make it compelling:

Mandatory details:

Scope:

SIR JOHN HEGARTY

Friends of Jörg

Chairman,
Worldwide Creative Director,
Bartle Bogle Hegarty

Turning Intelligence into Magic: A Case for Creativity

"How many impressions? Did awareness go up? How does it compare to the competition?"

These days, marketers seem to have fallen in love with measuring the success of their advertising—spurred on by the Internet and its measurable clicks, the old adage of "half of my advertising money is wasted, I just don't know which half" is no longer true. Clients ask for effectiveness and efficiency, and rightfully so. Marketing communications is where art meets business, it is bound to achieve tangible results.

But the main ingredient that will help achieve the goals that have been set is still creativity. Now, more than ever, any piece of communication needs an idea: An idea that can help it stand out and cut through the increasing clutter of messages. An idea that can touch people's hearts and connect them to the brand. An idea based on some universal human truth, an observation that is true in London and Sao Paulo, in Singapore and Shanghai.

So after the planner has found the one insight, one observation, moulded into a truly single-minded proposition that will give the creative team a basis, a topic and a direction, the hardest job in any agency begins: Turning intelligence into magic. Finding new creative ways to express the insight, adding that sparkle, the element of surprise, the smile that helps us notice, understand, remember. And doing it again and again; always new, always different.

Discipline is also needed on the other side of the equation: Clients need to realise that their quest for numbers, the need to see awareness points and most-likely-to-use scores move up, has a time and place—after the campaign has run. They are right to expect the communication campaign to touch their consumers, to move them and change their minds.

But they need to remember that they hired an agency for a reason: Because they need the expert in discovering insights and crafting messages that will reach their target, will speak to them and hopefully leave a lasting impression. If the ideas used to get the message across are new and fresh, they could bomb in a pre-test. Because testing basically works like a rear-view-mirror: All over the world, consumers reference new campaigns against what they know and have seen before—so if the idea is original, there is little to compare it with, and consumers may be unsure how to judge it in a focus group situation. Instead, a brand that wants to be a leader needs to look forward, to constantly refresh. Also, clients need to understand that research is by far no exact science—much depends on the set-up and then the interpretation of results.

Clients need to trust their agency as much as they trust their surgeon: Both know what they are doing; they have the right tools to achieve results and they have their best interests at heart.

SIR JOHN HEGARTY

Friends of Jörg

Chairman,
Worldwide Creative Director,
Bartle Bogle Hegarty

John started in advertising as a junior Art Director at Benton and Bowles, London in 1965. He then joined a small Soho agency, John Collings & Partners, and in 1967 joined the Cramer Saatchi consultancy which became Saatchi & Saatchi in 1970, where he was a founding shareholder. One year later, he was appointed Deputy Creative Director.

John left in 1973 to co-found TBWA, London as Creative Director. The agency was the first to be voted *Campaign*'s (UK's leading advertising magazine) Agency of the Year in 1980.

In 1982 he left to start Bartle Bogle Hegarty (BBH) which was soon to become one of the most talked-about advertising agencies in the world. Four years later, in 1986, BBH was voted *Campaign* magazine's Agency of the Year, and won the title again in 1993, 2003, 2004 and 2005. In addition, BBH became the Cannes Advertising Festival's very first Agency of the Year in 1993 by winning more awards than any other agency. It won the title again in 1994. Most recently, BBH Worldwide was voted *Campaign* magazine's first ever Network of the Year at the end of 2004.

In the first two decades of BBH's history, John was responsible for famous campaigns for Levi's such as the famous 'Launderette' commercial starring an unknown model called Nick Kamen. He introduced the phrase *Vorsprung Durch Technik* for Audi which has become one of the UK's most famous advertising slogans. He was the first to pick a young model / actor called Brad Pitt to star in a commercial and he also pioneered the importance of music for Levi's. That resulted in the soundtracks from seven Levi's commercials getting to the UK number one spot.

BBH now has offices in London, New York, Singapore, Tokyo, Sao Paulo and Shanghai and Hegarty oversees the creative output of all BBH offices around the world. This unique global structure also contributed to the company winning the Queen's Award for Export Achievement twice, in 1996 and 1997.

Since setting up BBH, John's industry awards include two D&AD Golds and six Silvers, Cannes Golds and Silvers, and British Television Gold and Silvers. He was awarded the D&AD President's Award for outstanding achievement in the advertising industry and chaired the 1999 New York Art Directors Advertising Show. He has also been voted one of the most influential people in fashion. And the International Clio Awards awarded John, in May 2005, the very prestigious Life Time Achievement Award for his outstanding achievement in the industry. In October 2005, John was inducted into America's highly acclaimed and influential One Club's Creative Hall of Fame. Recently John has been awarded honorary Doctorates by both Middlesex University and Buckingham University respectively.

CAMPAIGN TITLE
WATERMELON / FROG / LIGHT BULB

CLIENT
Siam Tamiya

AGENCY
Creative Juice / G1 Co. Ltd.

AGENCY CREDITS

Thirasak Tanapatanakul – Executive Creative Director
Natchanun Chaiphanumas / Prangthip Praditpong – Copywriter
Thirasak Tanapatanakul / Kittitat Larppitakpong – Art Director

TIME FRAME OF CAMPAIGN

2005 – 2006

CAMPAIGN TITLE

Watermelon / Frog / Light Bulb

OBJECTIVES OF CAMPAIGN

Reinforce Tamiya's position – The 1st Choice of Assembly Toys

TARGET GROUP

Assembly toy lovers of all ages

COMMUNICATION STRATEGY

Use insight of the target group in our communication, to show that Tamiya is the brand for them.

CHOICE OF MEDIA

Magazine and Poster (Print)

CREATIVE EXECUTION

What assembly toy lovers see when they look at shattered objects.

RESULTS

Cannes Lion Award
Gold Lion (Print)
Silver Lion (Outdoor)

D&AD

Accepted in book

The One Show

Silver Pencil (Print)

CLIO Awards

Silver (Print Single & Campaign)
Bronze (Poster)
Finalist (Print & Poster)

A/P AdFest

Most Awarded Agency in Asia-Pacific
Best of Show (Print)
Gold (Print & Poster)

Media Asian Advertising Awards

Certificates of Excellence (Print)

AdMan Awards & Symposium (Thailand)

Gold (Print)

BAD: Bangkok Art Director's Awards

2 Certificates of Excellence (Print Single & Campaign)

FOR THOSE WITH
AN EYE FOR ASSEMBLY
TAMIYA

FOR THOSE WITH
AN EYE FOR ASSEMBLY
TAMIYA

FOR THOSE WITH
AN EYE FOR ASSEMBLY
TAMIYA

4. The right ad agency

There are hundreds of advertising agencies out there—specialised or full service; creative, strategic or both; small or big; below-the-line, above-the-line or through-the-line; interactive, local, global, award-winning and run-of-the-mill. It can be confusing to find out which is the right agency if you are a client, and it always helps to apply some criteria as the first filter before you decide whom to invite to pitch.

Track Record What have they done before? Do you like their work? Which clients have they worked for? Are they reputable in the industry? Do they have a reputation for being difficult or too award-focused? Feel free to check with their existing clients. Also, does the agency have experience in your segment? (You may want to work with an agency which knows the segment and players already; or you may want to choose an agency without segment experience who can look at your brief with fresh eyes and disrupt segment conventions.)

Size Are they the right size for you? You may be impressed by the big names, but if you're a medium-size client, it's probably better to be a big fish in a small pond instead of a small fish in the big client pool of a multinational network. Big fish get more attention and better people get to work for them. Big agencies sometimes have higher overheads, so working with the big names may turn out to be expensive for you.

Network Most businesses these days are multinational. That is why your agency needs to be where your target consumers are. Some small creative networks use a hub-and-spoke system by serving multiple locations from a regional hub. This is possible but represents a logistical challenge, especially if you need local language skills and media or government contacts.

Cash Can you afford them? You know your budget (if you don't, go to the chapter on budgeting for an ad campaign), so make sure that they understand your limitations and don't accept an agency or campaign that realistically you cannot afford. There is a myth in the agency world that if a client really likes the big idea, he will find the money to afford it, but it's less and less true in these days of measuring effectiveness and competing media.

Culture This point is related to the one about an agency's track record. You need to understand the agency's culture and this is something best gleaned from a personal visit to the agency office. After all, there are all kinds. You need to choose the one that is most in tune with your own culture. You probably don't want an agency that is in it purely for the money and will be your reliable 'yes-man' or 'yes-woman.' You want one to challenge you, to share its expert knowledge and opinion and to push you towards bolder campaigns that will cut through the clutter. Unlike you, it's not caught up in the corporate treadmill, so it can be (and should be) adding the right amount of guts and spine. On the other hand, you probably also don't want an agency that doesn't care about what you say (or about your brand, for that matter). Both are dangerous—the agency needs to be able to listen as well as talk and it needs to have the best interests of your brand at heart. Whether or not the campaign wins an award is important for the agency but secondary for you.

People

Communication is a people business, so you must choose the people you work with very carefully. After all, these are the people that you will see almost every day for years to come. If you don't like them, both your lives will be miserable and the work, as well as your brand, will suffer. Make sure that you meet the team that has been bookmarked to work on your account, not the creative director flown in from China or the strategic planner from London; they will fly off again tomorrow. Get to know the people, and see if you trust them and if you click. If you have a choice in the second step of the selection process to choose between an agency with the better idea but where you don't like the team, and one where you love the team but don't like the idea, choose the latter. They can always come up with another idea, or maybe you can buy the idea off the other team.

Conflict

You don't want your agency to work for your competitor. They may talk about firewalls or even different offices under one roof, but you may want a clear separation. It's just too dangerous. People talk. So if they work for the competition, they're off the list unless they are prepared to fire your competitor upon winning your account. That would free them up, but would you want to work with an agency that treats clients like that? If it happened to them, it could happen to you.

Specialisation Are they familiar with all the media that you need to employ to reach your target? While more and more agencies look at a 360-degree approach to advertising, some may specialise in online media, television commercials, etc. Make sure the agency you choose can handle the media you need.

Once you have screened all available agencies, shortlist a few and invite them to pitch. Basically, a pitch is a competition where all agencies are given the same brief. The brief is usually one that discusses how to communicate your brand positioning with clear parameters regarding objectives, message, timing, target, budget, etc. The agencies work on the brief independently and then present you with their respective strategies and campaigns. The point of this exercise is:

- you get to know the team
- you get an idea of how they think and whether they 'get' your brand
- you get an idea of their creative thinking potential

In the final presentation, you use the campaigns presented together with your impression of the people to decide which agency you want to appoint or sometimes, which two agencies you want to start negotiating price with. Be careful with the latter, however. If it's not handled carefully, it can damage the nascent relationship. Your appointment of an agency as a long-term partner should not depend solely on price. While you should be able to afford them, the financial aspect should be win-win with both sides happy and content. Feel free to go with your gut-feeling and stand up in a meeting and shout, "You've got it!" The team working on your project will have a great story to tell the other members when they get back to the office, and will reward you with loyalty and good work.

WHAT IF YOU'RE AN AGENCY? HOW DO YOU SELECT YOUR CLIENTS?

Sadly, while clients apply many different criteria to appoint the right agency, agencies sometimes work with just any client for the money. If New Business Development in agencies was left to CFOs, that would always be the case. But in order to have a happy team, develop successful work and be profitable, agencies should also develop some criteria to determine which clients and accounts they should go after or which invitations to accept:

Track Record Clients also have histories. If you're an agency CEO, feel free to talk to your peers and to call them up to ask about a client they have worked with before. How does the client treat its agencies—as suppliers or partners? Does its Request for Information (RFI) require the agency to be 'resourceful and flexible?' For example, some clients may claim that they don't have the money for professional models and request that you put your agency staff in the ad. Do they want you to be able to "work with a multiple -layered organisation with several stakeholders," which is just another way of saying that your creative work has to pass through many hierarchical layers? Do they have a long-term relationship with their agencies or do they change agencies often?

Creativity Does the client elect for daring and cutting-edge solutions only to have cold feet and opt for the safe option every time?

Budget Does the client have the budget for the campaign or agency? Do they pay fairly and on time? Can your agency make a profit on this account? You need to make a profit unless it is for the following reasons: You can use the brand name to attract other clients, the client allows you to do award-winning work that will help you attract good talent, it is good for your image or it's a charity and you're prepared to do some pro bono work because you believe in the cause.

In summary, agencies should look for the 3 Cs:

CASH, CULTURE, CREATIVITY

to determine whether a client is right for them.

SO NOW YOU, MR CLIENT, HAVE AN AGENCY.

Or do you? Before you start working together, there is just one more small issue to tackle: Money.

CAMPAIGN TITLE
A UNIQUELY AUSTRALIAN INVITATION
CLIENT
Tourism Australia
AGENCY
M&C Saatchi (Sydney)

CLIENT CREDITS
Ian Macfarlane, Director Marketing – Tourism Australia

AGENCY CREDITS
Tom Macfarlane, Regional Creative Director – Asia Pacific & America;
Ben Welsh, Creative Director – Sydney;
Michael Andrews, Head of Art – Sydney;
Marie Jackson, Managing Director – Sydney;
Tim McColl Jones, Global Group Head – Sydney

TIME FRAME OF CAMPAIGN
Progressive launches in Australia, Los Angeles, Berlin, London, Hong Kong, Shanghai, Beijing, Tokyo and Seoul from March 2006

CAMPAIGN TITLE
A Uniquely Australian Invitation

OBJECTIVES OF CAMPAIGN
To increase the 'active intention' for travel to Australia.

TARGET GROUP
Experience Seekers. A global audience with a common set of beliefs, values and travel motivators. They are well-educated, interesting, open-minded and acquire personal growth and self-fulfilment through travel. These people have a propensity to travel (especially long-haul) and spend money on new and different travel experiences.

PROPOSITION

Australia invites you to get involved.

COMMUNICATION STRATEGY

Mobilise Experience Seekers, convert Experience Seekers into brand advocates, address a single global target with a unified brand and communications message.

CHOICE OF MEDIA

Television, Cinema, Digital, Magazine, Out-Of-Home

CREATIVE EXECUTION

"So, Where the Bloody Hell Are You?"

COUNTRIES COVERED

Key source markets in Asia, Japan, the UK, the US, Europe and New Zealand

RESULTS

The campaign created a huge amount of PR globally given its uniquely Australian expression and tone.

Millions of people from more than 200 countries have seen the commercial; particularly through digital means.

An improvement in key brand tracking measures.

THE RUNWAY'S BEEN WORLD HERITAGE LISTED.
THE KAYAKS HAVE BEEN UNLOADED.
AND YOU CAN PADDLE OR JUST GO WITH THE FLOW.
SO WHERE THE BLOODY HELL ARE YOU?
Australia.com

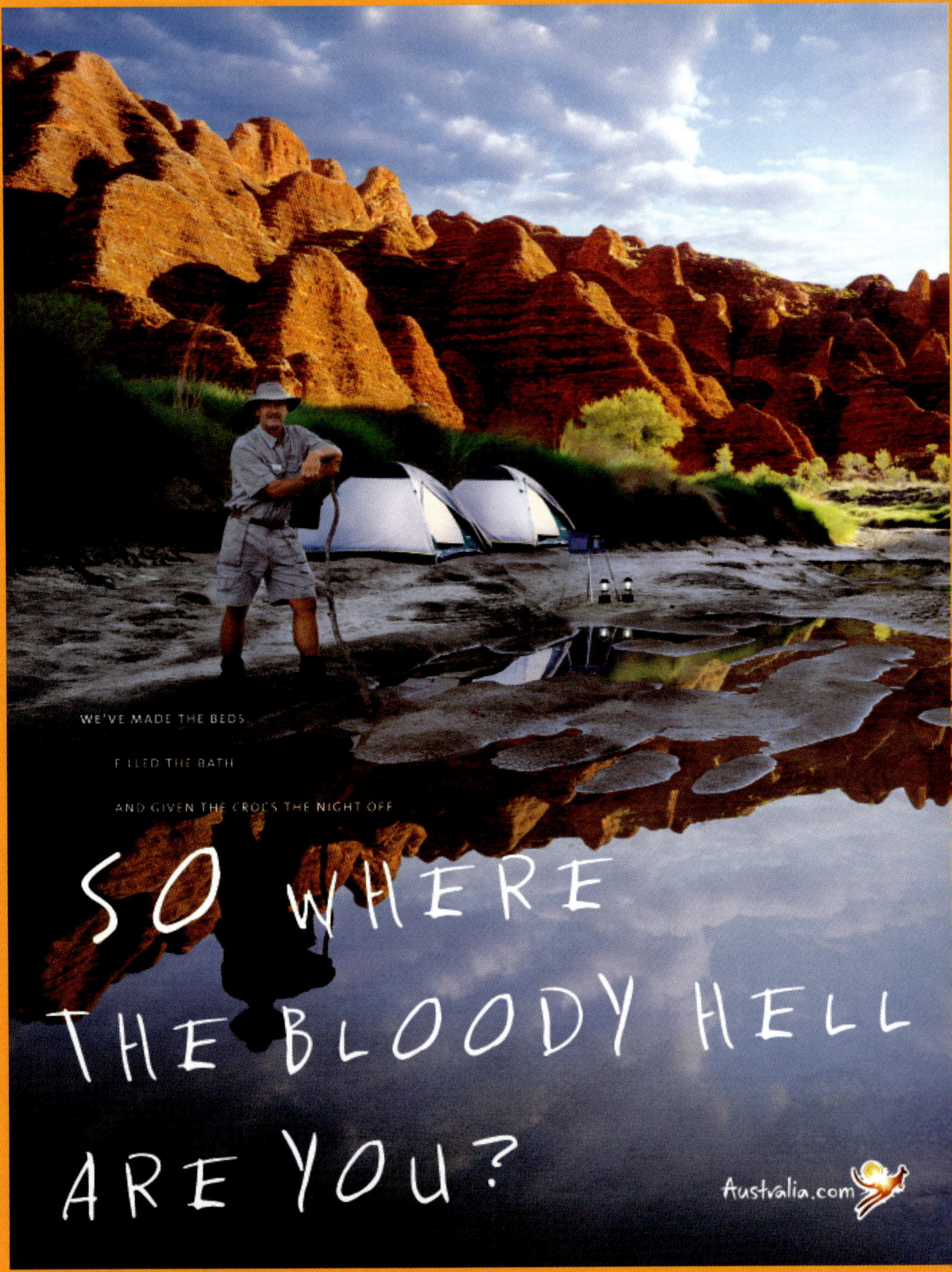
WE'VE MADE THE BEDS,
FILLED THE BATH
AND GIVEN THE CROCS THE NIGHT OFF
SO WHERE THE BLOODY HELL ARE YOU?
Australia.com

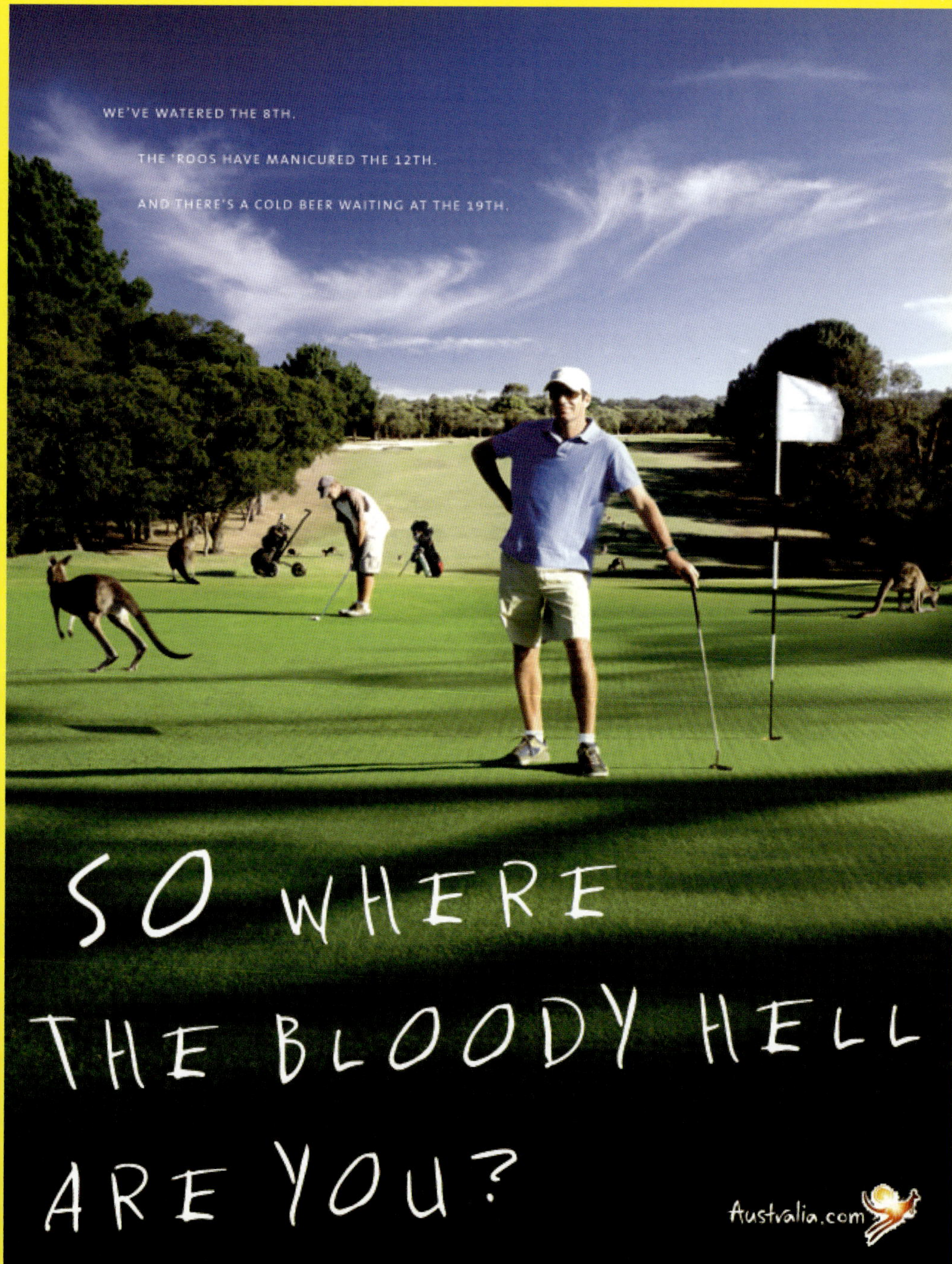
WE'VE WATERED THE 8TH.
THE 'ROOS HAVE MANICURED THE 12TH.
AND THERE'S A COLD BEER WAITING AT THE 19TH.
SO WHERE THE BLOODY HELL ARE YOU?
Australia.com

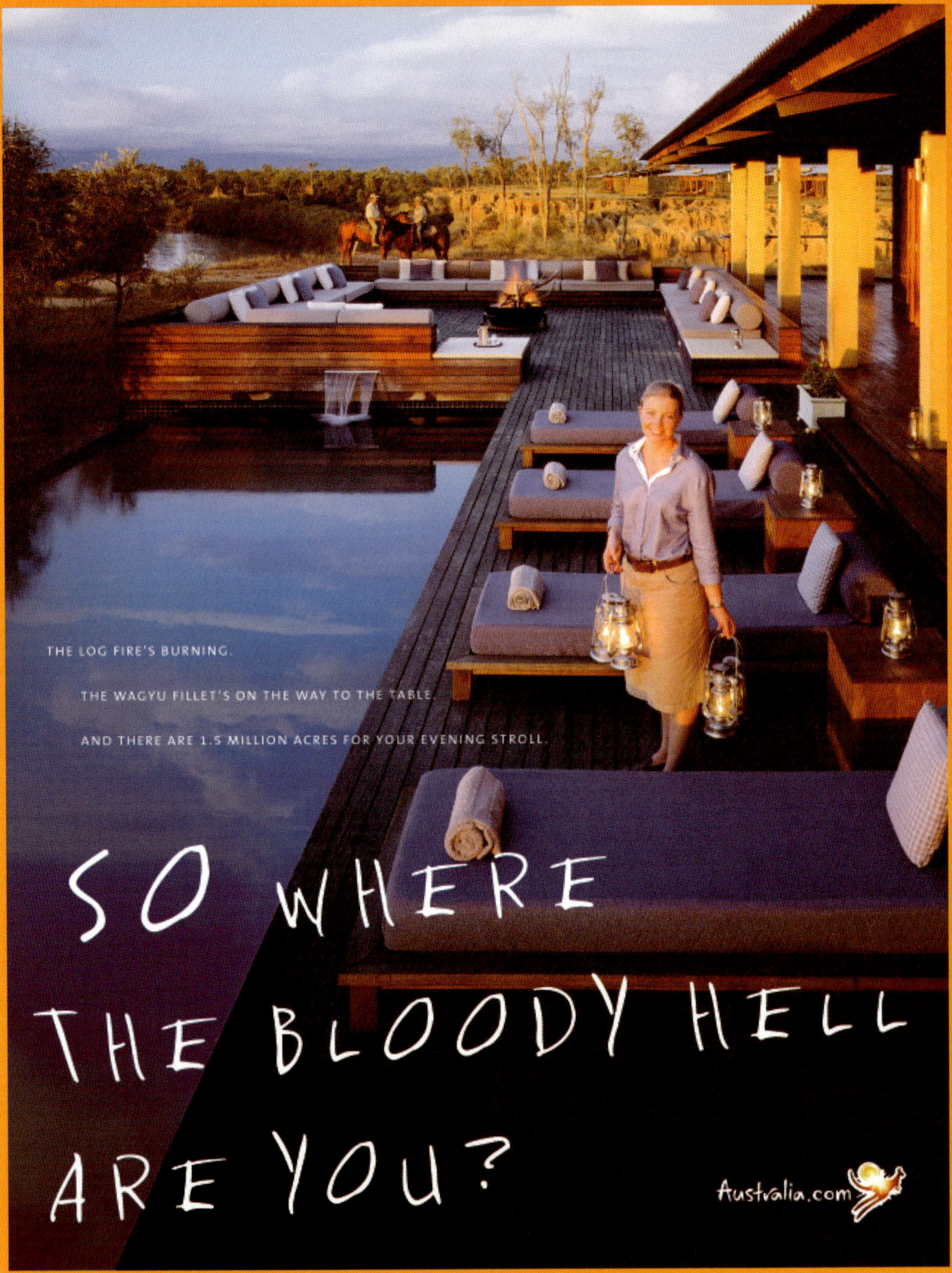
THE LOG FIRE'S BURNING.
THE WAGYU FILLET'S ON THE WAY TO THE TABLE.
AND THERE ARE 1.5 MILLION ACRES FOR YOUR EVENING STROLL.
SO WHERE THE BLOODY HELL ARE YOU?
Australia.com

Tourism Australia—
"Where the bloody
hell are you?"
TVC – 60s

5. How should you pay your ad agency?

It's funny that a business at the forefront of modern culture can be so conservative and change-averse inside. In many agency-client relationships, the way the agency is paid has not changed for over a hundred years.

IMAGINE THIS:

SCENARIO: An early newspaper, somewhere in the US, late 1800s. It carries local news, some national stories, and also announcements by the stores in town about what they are selling and any special offers. People at the paper put together these first 'ads' which are mostly no more than naming the store, its products and its address. The butcher, hairdresser and greengrocer are paying the paper a fee for these small ads. Then a clever typesetter at the paper has a genius business idea.

He knows how to use type and can produce much better-looking ads than the current ones. So he talks to the paper's owner and says, "How about I put together those cumbersome ads for you, and I also liaise with the local businesses so you and your staff can concentrate on producing the newspaper? I will bring in more ads than before so the paper will earn more money!" "Good idea", replies the newspaper owner. "I will give you a commission if you save me so much work and time. How about 15% of the price we charge the greengrocer?" "Deal!" says the typesetter and then goes to meet the local business owners.

"Here is my proposition", he says to the butcher. "Let me create your ad for you. I will make it look better than before, because I am an expert at typesetting. You will only have to deal with me, nobody at the newspaper's. And the best thing: It's free, you just pay me what you used to pay the paper." "What's not to like?", replies the butcher. And the greengrocer. And the hairdresser. "Deal!"

And to this day, this is how many ad agencies are still being paid. They get a percentage, as commission, of the media spending. True, these days, they will have to share it with the media agencies, ever since the great unbundling of media some years ago. And true, the percentage is often less than 15% depending on the size of the overall budget. But every day, agencies across the globe from London to Barcelona, and New York to Dusseldorf are being paid based on this ancient system.

PAYMENT BY MEDIA COMMISSION

For the creative agency, there is no direct relationship between their work, time spent and the media budget. It takes the same effort to produce one TV commercial, regardless of whether it runs once or 100 times.

The Media Temptation

If the payment is linked to the overall amount the client spends for media buying (i.e. it's not media-neutral); it gives an incentive to the agency to make the client spend more since that will mean more income for the agency. Even if it's the right move for the brand, it's hard to recommend spending less money in traditional media and more, say, in Direct Marketing (DM) if your agency's bottom line depends on it.

Another problem with linking agency payment to media commission is that it makes it harder for agencies to plan since budgets can change. If there's a drop in the client's business, the media budget can be increased to boost sales with an advertising campaign or it can be cut in order to save costs. Most marketers know advertising should be anti-cyclical, but it's hard to be so when your media budget is your only budget that is relatively painless to cut. If the media budget gets cut by half in the middle of the year, the agency faces a dilemma: They will still have to work for the client while having to pay the team handling the business with half the income.

The Award Temptation

Agencies want to win awards, which is fair and right. Winning awards helps agencies raise their profile. Awards help them to win new business and attract talent, not just in the creative department but across the board. Just make sure that your agency suggests what's right for the brand and does not put forth campaign ideas that are award-worthy but which could harm your brand. Align yourself with the planners and account managers who should have a good idea about your business and what it needs.

PAYMENT BY MAN-HOURS

For media-agencies, the commission system makes more sense since their work—media-planning and buying—is more directly related to the overall amount you spend.

So is there a better way to pay creative agencies?

Of course there is. The ideal solution for payment should be based on the one measurement that is used in most transactions: Time.

The client outlines the business problem he has, and the agency proposes a solution that will include a number of ads in different media. From its experience, the agency can estimate how many people it would take to run the account—from account management to planning to creative.

Once a client agrees on the team, the agency can calculate the cost based on the salaries of the staff.

This determines the overall cost of the people directly involved in the account. But would all these people spend 100% of their time working for this one client? Probably not:

- One of the advantages of working in the planning or account management team of an advertising agency is the fact that one is exposed to more than one brand; most of the time, agency staff are working for different brands from different categories at the same time. They find this fun because there's more to learn and work is never boring.

- Creatives need to stay fresh and keep thinking about different topics and brands to come up with original ideas. If they work for the same brand exclusively for a long time, they may run out of ideas or burn out quickly. Give them the stimulation of working for different brands and they stay fresh. Also, this allows the agency to get creatives to work on brands that are not so glamorous and that perhaps have a lower chance of winning awards. Working on less popular accounts can be 'tolerated' by the creative teams if, as compensation, they get to work occasionally for the 'cool' brands, too.

- There are clients who want at least part of their account management team to be 'dedicated', committing 100% of their time and effort. This makes sense if your business is complicated and you need to develop some 'brand experts' on the agency side who really understand the intricacies of what you do. (It also allows possessive clients to check on the whereabouts of 'their' agency staff since they have no reason to be 'away' or 'in another meeting' if they're 100% dedicated.) If so, the agency would most likely assign staff from the mid levels since lower levels are put on different accounts to learn more and higher levels have a supervisory role.

So you think you pay the team's salaries and that's all? Well, how about the tea lady? And the CEO? And the HR department? Most general and administrative functions will not be included in the direct salaries, but you will need to pay your share. How much these overheads will cost you varies from agency to agency and location to location. In many cases, the amount calculated for overheads matches 100% of the direct salaries.

If all clients paid the salaries of their direct team plus overheads, the agency would survive but not grow. So far we have not included agency profits in our calculations. However, most networks mandate a 15% or so Year-On-Year (YOY) growth for every local office. You may not agree to that, but most of the time the agency would come back with a calculation which looks something like this:

AGENCY TEAM FOR CLIENT A

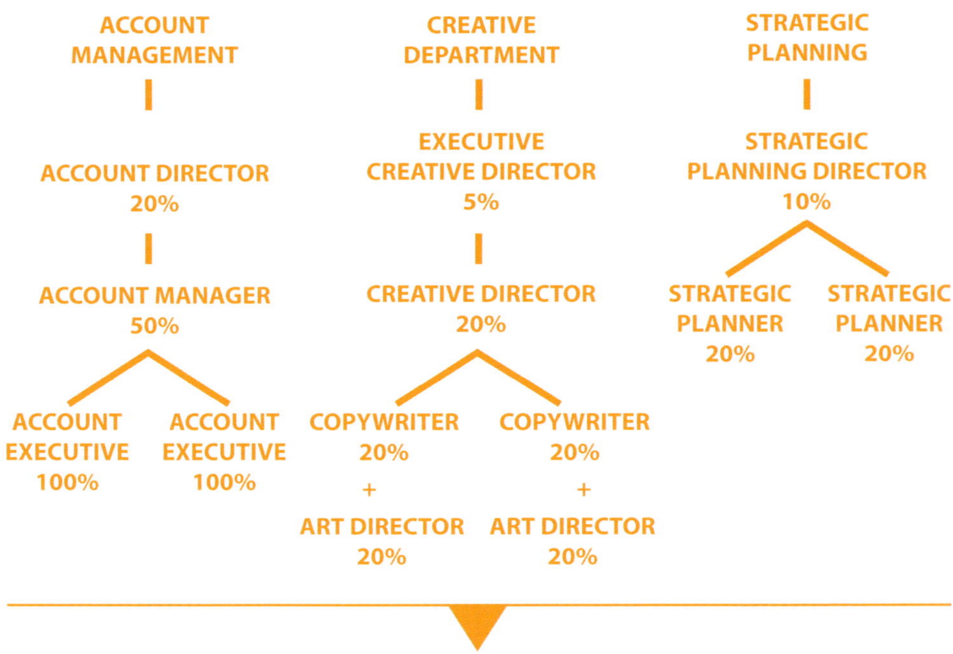

(100%) Salaries + (100%) Overheads + (15% to 20%) Profit

You can then start to negotiate and question the overheads percentage and the profit margin until you agree on a number that both sides are happy with. Remember, win-win. If you squeeze your agency on the terms too hard, they may agree in the short run, but you won't get a happy and motivated team in the long run. In the end, the agency may start looking for a better paying client.

PAYMENT BY RESULTS

In recent years, performance has been a buzzword floating around the agency scene. Clients are getting more demanding and want more value for money. They want to see real results and are prepared to pay for them. Some developments in the media scene have reacted to that. They mostly comprise new channels via the Internet, which allows for much more measurable results. With these new systems, clients only pay when consumers click on an online ad and, sometimes, only when they spend a certain amount of time on the website or when an actual sale is made.

For more traditional ways of advertising, such as TV and print ads, it's more complicated to introduce payment by results. The question is: What results? The easy answer—sales—does not work. No agency head in his or her right mind will agree to agency payment tied to sales figures because sales are influenced by a myriad other factors that advertising cannot influence. What if it rains and consumers stay at home during the campaign period? What if the competitor drastically reduces his price and destroys the impact of a perfectly orchestrated advertising campaign? What if the ad creates awareness and even stimulates trial but the consumers cannot find the product because there is a problem with distribution?

The key to payment by results is to consider these :

- determine what results a campaign can realistically achieve. A rise in awareness, increase in top-of-mind (TOM) unaided recall and sympathy are some parameters that advertising can influence.
- determine what is the target for the planned increase. You need to conduct a pre-campaign measurement in order to find out what your awareness or TOM scores are before the campaign. After this is done, you determine the level of TOM increase you want to realistically achieve, and then you measure the effectiveness after the campaign is over. There should be a gap between measurements to allow for a time lag between the point when consumers see the message in an ad and the time when it actually sinks in and the ad is played back to a focus group.
- recognise that this testing is necessary but it costs money. You will need to determine who is to pay for it—the agency or the client.
- finally, make the 'payment-by-results' a small part of the overall compensation scheme. Experience has shown that it is best used for

the top 5% or so of the overall remuneration. This gives the agency an incentive to reach a full 100% upon reaching the pre-agreed targets.

- you can make part of the 'payment-by-results' dependent on agency performance, based on an annual or bi-annual evaluation. Do not abuse this tool and make sure your evaluation is fair and transparent and not driven by your desire to save costs. When you budget for agency compensation, always budget for the full possible amount. If you want your agency to be successful in order to help you build your brand, you need to be prepared to reward them for it.

CAMPAIGN TITLE
KINETIC V4

CLIENT
Kinetic Singapore

AGENCY
Kinetic Singapore

AGENCY CREDITS
Creative Director – Sean Lam

TIME FRAME OF CAMPAIGN
From September 2006

CAMPAIGN TITLE
Kinetic V4

OBJECTIVES OF CAMPAIGN
As Kinetic Singapore's online front, this web site serves as an introduction to the agency, and a platform for showcasing their work. As such it is suitably wacky, given Kinetic's penchant for breaking with convention. The starship, intergalactic theme that is such a trademark of Kinetic is further evolved in this site, with the starship transforming into a robot out to vanquish bad advertising!

TARGET GROUP
Business requiring a fun and creative way of communication.

PROPOSITION
Break the convention with Kinetic.

CHOICE OF MEDIA
Web site (Online)

COUNTRIES COVERED
Worldwide

RESULTS

Creative Circle Award 2005

Interactive: Corporate Image, Business-to-Business—Gold
Client: Kinetic Singapore
Title: Kinetic V4

Interactive: Craft–Art Direction—Gold
Client: Kinetic Singapore
Title: Kinetic V4

Interactive: Craft–Illustration—Silver
Client: Kinetic Singapore
Title: Kinetic V4

Interactive: Craft–Soundtrack / Music / Effect—Silver
Client: Kinetic Singapore
Title: Kinetic V4

Interactive: Craft–Animation (2D and 3D)—Silver
Client: Kinetic Singapore
Title: Kinetic V4

Interactive: Craft–Writing—Bronze
Client: Kinetic Singapore
Title: Kinetic V4

Interactive: Craft–Typography— Bronze
Client: Kinetic Singapore
Title: Kinetic V4

Asia Interactive Awards 2006

Web site: Best Use Of Illustration—Gold
Client: Kinetic Singapore
Title: Kinetic V4

Web site: Best Self-Promotion Web site—Gold
Client: Kinetic Singapore
Title: Kinetic V4

Web site: Best Use of Animation—Silver
Client: Kinetic Singapore
Title: Kinetic V4

Asia Pacific Advertising Festival 2006

Web site: Business-to-Business—Silver
Client: Kinetic Singapore
Title: Kinetic V4

British D&Ad Awards 2006

Digital Crafts (Art Direction)—Silver Nomination
Client: Kinetic Singapore
Title: Kinetic V4

Digital Crafts (Animation and Motion Graphics)—Silver Nomination
Client: Kinetic Singapore
Title: Kinetic V4

CLIO Awards 2006

Web site: Self-Promotion—Silver
Client: Kinetic Singapore
Title: Kinetic V4

Communication Arts 12th Annual Advertising Exhibition

Category—Self- Promotion—Award of Excellence
Client: Kinetic
Title: Kinetic V4

The One Show Interactive 2006

For Excellence in New Media Advertising (Self- Promotion)—Merit
Client: Kinetic Singapore
Title: Kinetic V4

KiNETiC
WHAT'S UP
THIS IS KINETIC
MEET THE CREW
OUR WORK
VICTORIES
MAKE CONTACT
HOMEPAGE
© copyright 2005. Kinetic Singapore

KiNETiC
THE CREED
We fully intend to wipe bad advertising and design off the face of this planet and free its citizens from the mind-numbing properties of bad ads and ho-hum websites. Why can't websites be designed differently, with a bit of thought and a dash of flair? Why can't ads be thought-provoking, inventive and entertaining in equal measure?
ORIGINS
PHILOSOPHY
THE FUTURE
WHAT'S UP
THIS IS KINETIC
MEET THE CREW
OUR WORK
VICTORIES
MAKE CONTACT
HOMEPAGE
© copyright 2005. Kinetic Singapore

KINETIC
WE CAME
WE SAW
WE CONQUERED
1999
SINGAPORE CREATIVE CIRCLE AWARDS
Relationship Marketing (Websites) - Bronze
Client: Pestbusters Pte Ltd
Title: PestMobile
2000
ONE SHOW INTERACTIVE, NEW YORK
New Media Advertising (Website) - Gold
Client: Concave Scream
Title: Bandwidth Concave
New Media Advertising (Website) - Bronze
Client: Pestbusters Pte Ltd
Title: PestMobile
New Media Advertising (Website) - Merit
WHAT'S UP
THIS IS KINETIC
MEET THE CREW
OUR WORK
VICTORIES
MAKE CONTACT
HOMEPAGE
© copyright 2005. Kinetic Singapore

KINETIC
INTERACTIVE
DESIGN
ADVERTISING
TVCs AND MORE
WHAT'S UP
THIS IS KINETIC
MEET THE CREW
OUR WORK
VICTORIES
MAKE CONTACT
HOMEPAGE
Aamer Taher Design Studio
Ad Planet Group
Affixen
Calibre
Citibank
Filmworks Collective
Group Lotus
Heineken
Honda (Kah Motor)
Jubes
Lorgans the Retro Store
Motorola
Nokia
The Berth By The Cove
The Linear
The Observatory
The Picture Farm
We Love House
Yellow Box Studios
Change the rules
Welcome to Group Lotus PLC
Group Lotus
2004
The challenge was to organise and manage the huge amount of information required to go on this global site – and still keep the design and navigation super
© copyright 2005. Kinetic Singapore

6. Working with your ad agency

Client-agency co-operation is a people-business that requires strong people-skills on both sides. Agency staff, particularly creatives, are often very sensitive and need to be shown reward and understanding. Sometimes they even need to be pampered.

Overall, the client will get the best result from his agency if he treats the agency as a partner and respects its specialist knowledge and skills. The great thing about advertising is that everybody and their dog love it, watch it and have an opinion about it. But while no patient would tell his brain surgeon how to operate, clients often think they know better than the agency.

Okay, okay, it's no brain surgery nor rocket science, but the rule still stands: If you buy a dog, let it bark; don't do the barking. Let the agency do their job and give them space to do it. Let them feel that you take them seriously as your partner, not as a 'supplier'. Unfortunately, some big clients let their procurement departments handle the agency selection, with the effect that the agency will always be a supplier. But if you treat your agency staff well and give them respect, they will make an effort to be worthy of your praise by learning more about your business and giving you more thought-through, tailored solutions.

So you have determined, discussed and agreed on how to pay your agency. You can now start working with the agency. Let's have a look at the whole process from initial brief to seeing the final ad in a magazine or on TV:

1. Client Brief
2. Planning
3. Creative Brief
4. Creative Development
5. Client Approval
6. Execution
7. Media

So here we go: The client briefs the agency and the strategic planner looks into consumer behaviour and target group insights. He then develops the creative brief based on these, the creative team develops the work, the client approves it, the work gets produced and is finally put on air.

WHAT'S WRONG WITH THIS PICTURE?

A number of things: First of all, it is not so straightforward. There are often some loops involved (ideas/concepts that are developed but have to be refined and presented again), especially when it comes to the planning process. The strategic planner may have to make several loops until the client agrees to the creative brief. The client needs to agree to this since it will be the benchmark that the creative work will be measured against later. It helps, when appraising the idea, to move away from subjective judgement such as "I don't like it" to "Is it answering the brief that we all agreed to?" The creative team may also need to make some internal loops until everybody feels that the work is ready for client presentation. The client may reject the work a few times. Sometimes, under time-pressure, he agrees to production and hopes for the best.

There are many overlaps in the process:

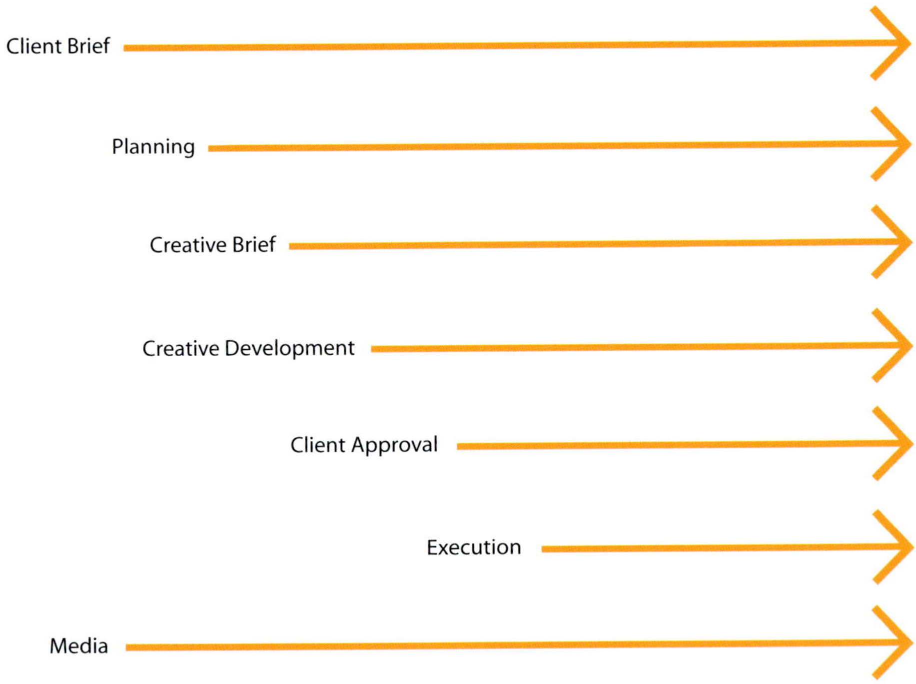

The strategic planner needs to stay involved and constantly check the developing work against the brief. A clever agency will involve the client at all times and have 'tissue' meetings (i.e. interim meetings where rough concepts are presented) to give sneak peaks and make sure they are on the right track.

Media planners also need to be involved right from the beginning. These days, with an ever-changing and growing media environment, media planners have become specialists and experts who hold information that account managers, strategic planners and creatives may not. Media owners approach them all the time with new advertising formats such as how one might now be able to buy up the whole front page of a local newspaper or use a new building as an advertising canvas for a short period, much like the branding campaign launched by *The Financial Times* on the new IFC2 tower in Hong Kong during its construction. This information needs to be shared with the creative team at the beginning of the process so they can create content to fit these formats. Unfortunately, this is not always done. The main reason for this is:

THE BIG MEDIA UNBUNDLING

Many years ago, this was how an average advertising agency was structured:

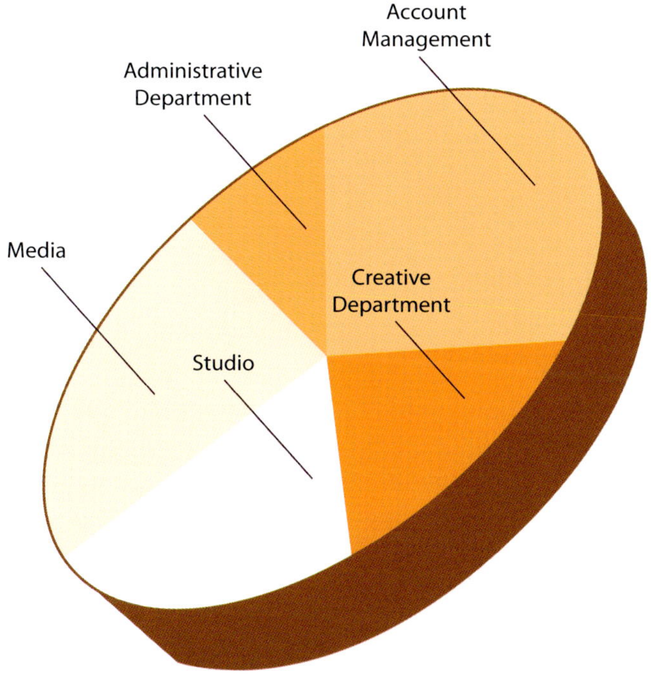

It would comprise the account management department, administration, the creative department, the studio and the media department. If the agency was in the UK or the US, it would have a small strategic planning department as well. Often, it was run independently by the founder or founders in one office location.

But with client demands and globalisation, agencies found that they had to internationalise and open offices in new markets to be where their clients were. That was when the first agency networks were born. Subsequently, holding companies were formed; they saw a good business opportunity and acquired most of the existing networks. Some of the larger holding companies today are:

- Omnicom (owns BBDO, DDB, TBWA, etc.)
- WPP (owns Ogilvy, JWT, Y&R, Red Cell, etc.)
- Interpublic Group (owns McCann, etc.)
- Publicis Groupe (owns Publicis, Saatchi & Saatchi, BBH, Leo Burnett, etc.)
- Dentsu

Most of the time, the agencies in one holding company work independently and competitively, and hold their own unique positioning so that there would be no client conflict. At the same time, this gives the holding company more opportunities to win a pitch because more of its agencies can be represented. Individual agencies are often part of multinational agency networks owned by the big holding companies. Clients usually move on the network-level, i.e. they choose an agency network to do their regional or global work. Rarely does a client approach a holding company asking it to put together a global solution, although one famous example was in 2004 when HSBC awarded its more than US$400,000,000 account to Martin Sorrell's 'Dream Team' from different WPP agencies.

As holding companies are driven by revenue growth, it's natural that they look at avenues for increasing profits and cutting costs. The result has been 'media unbundling' as they move the media departments out of their existing agencies and consolidate them into one or more media companies, like OMD (Omnicom), Zenith and Mindshare (WPP) or Starcom (Publicis). This has the following advantages:

- Media agencies can now work for the combined clients of all agencies.
- There are greater discounts from media owners because of the larger volume.
- Running costs are reduced as there is no duplication of functions.
- Media agencies are now able to accept assignments from clients outside their agency networks.

So, who benefits?

- Clients: For the very first time, they have a choice in who plans and buys their media. They also receive better discounts.
- Holding companies: Their income has increased.
- Media agencies: With a new size and independent clients, there is new confidence in the agencies that have not always been treated with the respect they deserve.

But there is also a downside for consumers and clients:

- Media experts who now have their own (independent) clients will, with their new-found confidence, allow these clients to take priority.
- Account management do not involve the media planners as early as they used to since they are no longer based in the same location. What results is that media is now simply handed the final creative and asked to place it. Not enough time or effort is put into exploring new formats that may benefit clients and consumers—since it's no longer a case of walking down the corridor and finding a sympathetic media planner.

Fortunately, the problems have been recognised, and there are now discussions about moving at least part of the media back into the agency.

AGENCY FAMILY TREE

WPP GROUP	PUBLICIS GROUPE	OMNICOM GROUP	INTERPUBLIC GROUP OF COS.	HAVAS	DENTSU
ASATSU-DK	BARTLE BOGLE HEGARTY	BBDO	FCB	ARNOLD	DENTSU
BATES ASIA	FA LON	DDB	LOWE	EURO RSCG	
GREY	LEO BURNETT	TBWA	MCCANN ERICKSON	MPG*	
JWT	PUBLICIS	OMD*	INITIATIVE MEDIA*		
OGILVY & MATHER	SAATCHI & SAATCHI				
Y&R	ZENITH OPTIMEDIA*				
MINDSHARE*	STARCOM MINDVEST GROUP*				

*MEDIA SPECIALIST

Wow—they asked me to pick a celebrity (because I am the youngest). When I was 15, what magazines did I read, which TV programmes did I watch? Easy. I love the Japanese groups on VH1. And Korean soap operas. Even now. Hee Hee…
I know. I have one child myself. Children love celebrities. So I told Wu to find one for us. Everybody will notice! And my friends will congratulate me. Can even be a Taiwanese celebrity...I don't mind!

WILSON CHOW

Friends of Jörg

Associate Executive Creative Director, Ogilvy & Mather, Beijing

The Paradise for Adventurers

At the beginning of the previous century, Shanghai was known to be 'the paradise for adventurers'. But when I arrived around the end of that century, she was far from being a paradise for anyone. In fact it's more like hell for someone like me, an art director from New York.

It was a time when China was still trying to fit in with the rest of the world and advertising was taking her first baby steps. It was a time when everything in China had to be cheap, and the perception was that advertising production budgets should be small, if not be free at all.

It was also a time when most Chinese were eager to get in touch with foreigners, foreign trend and foreign things. 'Imported' practically meant 'best' and to be able to go abroad was like a dream come true. Advertising was still educating consumers on the benefit or usage of a product. The consumers in return became sponges and absorbed everything they could because the Internet was not that widely available.

It's a very different picture in China today. The explosion of Internet usage is probably one of the most important factors for all the changes. The Chinese no longer need to wait for anyone to inform them about the latest trend on anything. Online activities have created more Chinese trends, content and even celebrities than ever before. Traditional media are being challenged to a point where there are discussions in presentations where they are being omitted from the plan. More and more clients are waking up to this new age and it is necessary for our business to be able to provide the freshest solutions.

Welcome to China's 'Paradise for the ad adventurers'. This is a market for those who'll venture outside the norm. Successful campaigns no longer have only TV and print ads. In fact, there are times when these two media only become the support for other innovative media. It also means that creatives have to find new ways to produce or express their ideas. We can no longer afford to think that Chinese audiences lag behind their counterparts in the West. We need to realise that they are just as hip and cool and deserve the same calibre in terms of ideas, innovation and quality of production.

The good news is that the basic principle of an idea doesn't change. It still needs to be fresh, simple and entertaining. In fact, it is even more important to have an engaging idea than ever before. The audiences are no longer at the receiving end of a marketing campaign. A successful campaign will have the audiences take an active role and empower them to contribute to the communication. And just like the good old days, you will be rewarded with riches and glory if you do it right and you might lose your shirt if you don't. The key is, are you brave enough?

WILSON CHOW

Friends of Jörg

Associate Executive Creative Director, Ogilvy & Mather, Beijing

I was born and raised in Hong Kong for most of my teen years and was then packed and shipped to San Francisco when I turned 16. Most of my time spent in Hong Kong was quite unremarkable, except I was proud to say that I was among the few in this city of six million that knew about Duran Duran before they had ever hit the American Top 40. It was the 80s, so forgive me.

My time in the US was truly an eye opener for someone who had spent most of his childhood in a Christian boys' school. Unknowingly, I had ended up in the No 1 party school in America at the time. You only need to rent the movie 'Animal House' and you'll have a pretty good idea of what my life was like back then.

After college, I thought it might be a good idea to go to art school to learn how to make big bucks with my scribbling. After a semester or two, I discovered that advertising was where clients like Nike and Jeep would pay top dollars to make scribbles like mine come to life. It was an epiphany.

A teacher told me once, "If you can make it in New York, you can make it anywhere."

He has probably learned the line from a movie and just wanted to use it on a student.

Guessed it worked. I packed up my bags after graduation and went to New York city.

After spending a few years learning the ropes, I ended up in BBDO as an art director. But at the same time, I was going through a horrible break-up. So I decided to move to another place to continue my career and my life.

Shanghai seemed to be far enough and exotic enough. So, once again, I packed my bags and ventured to a brand new place.

China turned out to be a much longer stay than I had anticipated. After churning out some interesting work plus the first Cannes TV advertising finalist for China, I ended up in Berlin with DDB to work on Volkswagen.

But I missed San Francisco and my family.

In 2001, I went home and was just in time to see the September 11 tragedy happen. I can still remember every second of that morning.

The world has been a different place since then and I thought it might be a good idea to go back to China because that's where things were happening.

As it turned out, I was right about that. I have not moved again since then and I am happily working for Ogilvy Beijing on Moto.

CAMPAIGN TITLE
TIGER—UNRAVEL THE SECRET

CLIENT
Asia Pacific Breweries, Tiger Beer

AGENCY
Leo Burnett Asia Pacific

TIME FRAME OF CAMPAIGN

2005 – 2007

CAMPAIGN TITLE

Tiger—Unravel the Secret

OBJECTIVES OF CAMPAIGN

- Rebuild consumer perceptions of Tiger as a big international brand
- Re-establish logical credentials of Tiger to ensure consumers have a reason for purchase

TARGET GROUP

Males aged 25-45
Tiger "adoptors"

PROPOSITION

Every success must have a secret behind it; so this is the story behind Tiger's worldwide success. Let's tell the secret behind Tiger's worldwide success over 75 years in an engaging and creative way

COMMUNICATION STRATEGY

- Build a mechanism to get underneath the resistance of consumers to mass media advertising.
- Engaging story brings consumers into the brand, supported by facts told in an engaging way through other media.
- Extensive use of third party endorsement beforehand.

CHOICE OF MEDIA

- Built around 5 mini-films, this media tells the essence of the story, builds "wow" big brand perception.
- Internet movie-based approach, Directors' special cut of ads, plus interviews

- www.unravelthesecret.com
- Press/Magazine tells the logical story
- Outdoor ads and posters highlight salient facts closer to the product
- Third-party endorsement via PR

CREATIVE EXECUTION

- 6 films
- 8 press
- 5 outdoor/posters
- Web site
- Launch vehicle

COUNTRIES COVERED

Southeast Asia
Internet- worldwide (US, Europe, Australasia)

RESULTS

Allied to super cold campaign (another logical reason to believe)
Tiger sales increased 5% since campaign started in Singapore.

100,000 unique Internet views outside of Asia,
(visited site 3 times, viewed 1.5 ads per visit)

TIGER : UNRAVEL THE SECRET
unravelthesecret.com
Tiger

TIGER : UNRAVEL THE SECRET
unravelthesecret.com
Tiger

Tiger
EST.
1932
World Acclaimed
LAGER BEER

Tiger
EST. 1932
World Acclaimed
LAGER BEER
AWARDED CHAMPIONSHIP GOLD MEDALS: LONDON GENEVA PARIS

7. Advertising tools

What are some of the tools and themes that agencies employ when constructing a campaign? Be aware, though, that while some of these can help, they can also overshadow the message. Or they can be just an easy way out if there is a dearth of ideas.

CELEBRITIES

Some clients love to have celebrities in their campaigns. Shooting a print ad or TV commercial with these personalities gives them an opportunity to meet them. I have been to many clients' offices where the walls are framed with pictures showing the client smiling next to David Beckham, Zhang Ziyi or some other celebrity.

Celebrity endorsements can be useful as they help to:

- create instant awareness for a new product or service;
- position the brand by association;
- add credibility to the brand (Tiger Woods for golf clubs).

However, there is a potential downside to using celebrities as they can:

- overshadow the brand;
- reduce credibility if there is no link between their area of competence and the brand;
- become counterproductive when they are involved in some scandal (the Kate Moss-effect);
- also be expensive to use.

So every advertiser should consider very carefully if the personality traits of the celebrity match the brand or the product. Used carefully, celebrity advertising can help you position your brand and reach an impact that would be hard to achieve otherwise, as seen in the big sports brands such as Nike, adidas and VISA in Asia.

HUMOUR

Research has shown that people like funny ads and remember ads that make them smile. So humour can be a powerful tool to help give ads greater impact and make the ads more memorable. However, humour works on many levels. Make sure that the ads:

- are not offensive. Many people laugh at the misfortune of others, but that can backfire and position your brand in a negative way.
- are appropriate for your consumer. Some jokes travel, some don't. While most people—from those in living rooms in Manchester to those sitting in Indonesian ferries headed for Batam island—do understand the humour

of Mr Bean and laugh at his slapstick episodes, a subtle smile is often connected to local cultures and may not be understood elsewhere.

SEX APPEAL

Every semester, at the start of a new Advertising class, when I ask my students for their expectations of the course, one question inevitably pops up: Does sex really sell? There's no question that the use of sex in advertising is powerfully effective. There's a strong psychological appeal of sexual images used in print ads, online and in TV commercials. The interest is immediate, but if we decide to use sex to advertise our brand, we need to keep in mind a few caveats:

- Sexual imagery works better on men than on women. So we need to be clear who our target group is.
- You may alienate part of your audience: Some women find the use of the female body in advertising distasteful and inappropriate.
- If you plan to run your ad in more than one market, you have to make sure that local culture allows the showing of skin. In many markets, especially those with a strong religious base, there are strict rules about how much skin you can show.
- Make sure the image is appropriate for the message and your brand. Otherwise, people may remember the image but not what you want to say. Or you may raise awareness for your brand but fail to position it in the way you intended.

ENCODING/DECODING

Remember the discussion on how to communicate the positioning of the Brand You? We looked at the different tools that you have. These tools also stand for a code. Every time we communicate, we use a code involving at least one of these: language, speech, writing, colours, body language, symbols and music. Before we use these codes, we have to make sure that our target group can decode and understand our message.

This means that the recipients will have to be able to read and understand the language we're using, and have some idea what the symbols, colours, etc. that we reference stand for. This may be easy if you share the same culture, but as soon as you want your ad to work cross-culturally, you need to make sure that the code you use will be understood and that the interpretation is the one you intend. This concept of Cross-Cultural Communication shows how, even in the same market, you may talk to a target group that is different from you.

I love showing this chart to clients: It looks at the different fields of experience and illustrates how communication is more difficult if there is not much overlap between yourself and the target group. In my lectures, I sometimes reference songs from the 70s or 80s that my students, who are so much younger, have never heard of. Thus, my references don't work and I have to look for more recent examples from the overlap time period.

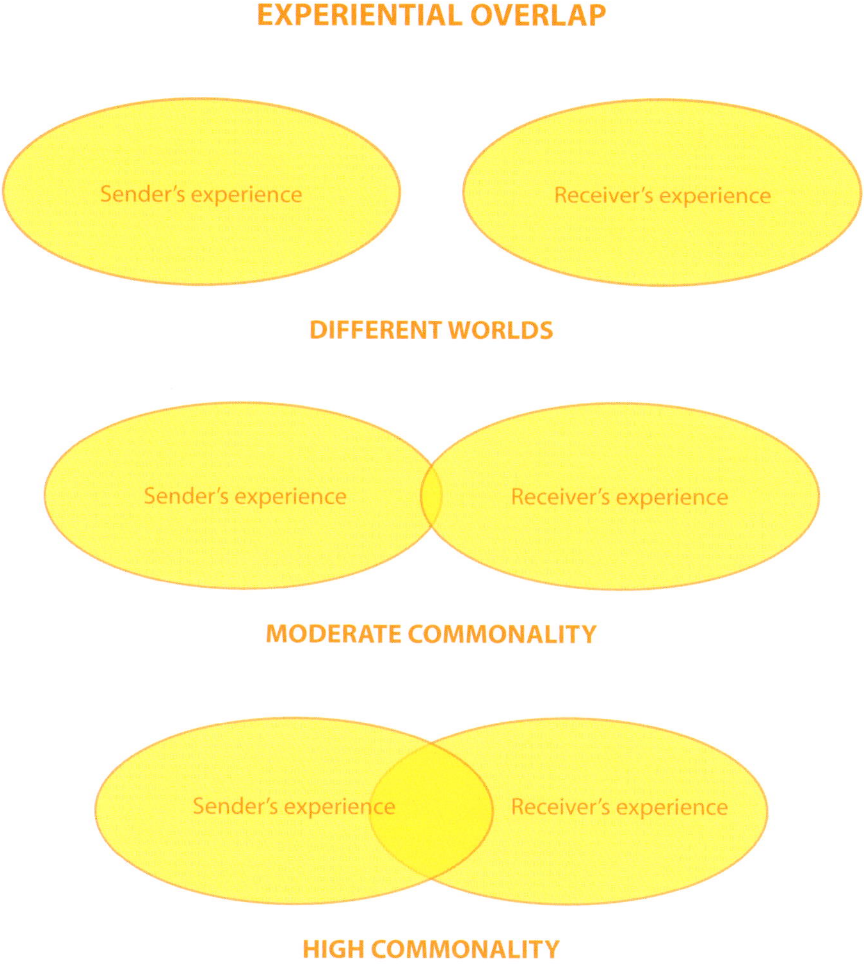

A few years ago, at BBDO, we produced a TV commercial for FedEx Asia-Pacific called 'Difficult Package'. It wanted to say how the FedEx team overcame obstacles with ingenious solutions because they went the extra mile for their customers – they lived to deliver. We used the code of a package that could run, jump and even fly to symbolise potential difficulties a shipment may run into (difficulty getting through customs, difficulty in locating the recipient, etc.). This commercial was well-received and understood in all markets in Asia except China. Subsequently, we found out through research that Chinese audiences, having only been recently exposed to advertising and thus had less time to learn how to decode sophisticated advertising messages, tended to take the story more literally. Instead of getting the message, they wondered, "What's in the package?" or "Is there a cat in the box?"

Also, when assessing creative work, clients should avoid the trap of thinking that they are the target and subsequently choose ads that appeal to them. Clients are never the target; most of the time they are not in the demographic and sociographic group that the ad wants to reach. Even if they are, they are still not a consumer because they work for the brand. They deal with it every day and look at communication for their brand through different eyes from the ordinary consumer.

In a recent presentation to Sony which was looking at ways to connect with their younger target groups, I started the presentation by showing two of the silliest videos from YouTube. Teens sometimes do things that don't make sense to adults—*bo liao,* they call this in local Hokkien. I showed these videos without introduction to my bewildered clients (most of them were in their late 20s to late 30s) and asked them, "Do you find this interesting? Is it funny?" Their answer was "No." Well, perhaps you may not find it funny, but your target will. So please bear in mind, when you look at creative ideas, that you are not the target."

A few months ago, my creative friend Andrew Lok asked me to give a short speech at Clients Meet Creatives, a gathering at Ogilvy Singapore. I used my five minutes and a few cue cards to make exactly that point:

Imagine there are some people who want to catch fish.
These are the fishermen. The fishermen are the clients.
The fish they want to catch are the consumers.

THE CLIENTS

THE IDEAS

THE CONSUMERS

But they need something to put on their fishing rod, something that will attract the fish to bite. They need worms. Worms are the ideas.

Where do the worms come from? From people who breed them and nurture them at work farms—the creatives.

So the worm farmers think about what the fish like and come up with the perfect worm. They give the worm to the fisherman; the fisherman looks at it and says: "I don't like it. I don't want to eat it."

"But it's not for you! You don't have to like it! It's for the fish! We know they will like it!" reply the worm farmers.

But the fisherman is unconvinced. So he gives the worm back and asks the worm farmers to come up with a better worm.

So, after a few similar experiences, the worm farmers realise that their best and juiciest worms won't make it to the fish since the fisherman doesn't like them. So they start breedings worms that won't appeal to the fish but to the fisherman. Nobody can live with constant rejection and frustration.

Exaggerated? Maybe. But clients need to realise that they are not the target. So the next time your agency presents you with some ideas that you don't like, look beyond your own taste and ask yourself: Would my target like it? If you're not sure, test them. The concept testing that we outlined, even with its limitations, may give you a better idea and some reassurance.

JIMMY LIANG

Friends of Jörg

Operations Director,
Leo Burnett Advertising,
Shanghai, China

Survival Kit in Advertising—An Account Management Perspective

Some years ago, a veteran in advertising whom I respect a lot said to me, "Advertising business is indeed quite a simple one—it is a business based on human emotions and confidence.'" I did not quite get it at the time.

Fortunately, I've learned a lot since then and come to appreciate the meaning. Put simply, I think there are seven points to becoming a better professional in the communication business:

- Be a listener
- Have trust and respect
- Be passionate
- Challenge yourself
- Take ownership and leadership
- Be agile to cope with changes
- Have fun and enjoy every moment

BE A LISTENER

Who on earth do you think understands your client's business issues best? The client himself. So listen to your clients—not just in the meeting room but also in informal situations. I find it most helpful when clients talk to me in private as a friend. They tend to tell me a lot more in-depth about their concerns, their sense of where the challenges lie, and their personal interest in connection with their business and organisation. Only when you really listen to them and understand what drives them as individuals, will you have won half the battle.

What about the other half? Just translate the issues into an action plan with your professional capability.

HAVE TRUST AND RESPECT

Advertising is no science. It is a hybrid comprising an understanding of consumer insight and the skills of taking advantage of marketplace reality and of applying military strategies. Which means that there is no absolute right or wrong.

Only when the clients believe that you have their business interests in mind always and see you as a valuable partner in the success formula, will you have a much better chance of making your clients appreciate what you sell—communication solutions.

The key thing here is that you need to earn the client's trust and respect over time. You have to carefully protect these equities. And you will be surprised by how much more you can achieve together with your clients if there is mutual trust and respect.

BE PASSIONATE

Advertising is a very enervating business, as is any business that draws on intellectual creativity. If you do not like what you are doing, you will drown very quickly with all the long hours, impossible deadlines and crisis in any given day.

Stay interested in what you do. Stay curious. Stay passionate.

CHALLENGE YOURSELF

In advertising we are only as good as our last idea, be it a creative idea, a thought to improve work efficiency, an insight into how consumers interact with a brand or product, or an innovative strategy to reach out to people. However, clients are always looking forward to see how we can better our last idea—rightly so in a creative industry.

We need to constantly challenge ourselves to go one up the next time—that is the only way we can improve our work and product.

TAKE OWNERSHIP AND LEADERSHIP

Have you ever wanted to tell your parents, your friends and your partner about your work? About how brilliant it is?

Only when you assume full ownership of your work and lead with responsibility will you have a better chance of producing work with excellent results. Then you can take pride in what you create and produce.

Be proud of what you contribute to the totality of your work. Pride is probably the best reward.

BE AGILE TO COPE WITH CHANGES

So long, farewell to the once television-dominated world. There have been many dramatic changes in the media landscape, consumer behaviour and in how consumers deal with the explosion of information. Thanks to the free economy, every consumer now has thousands, if not millions, of choices in every aspect of their daily lives.

These changes could be massive and sometimes deadly but as communication practitioners, we must not be afraid to deal with the increasingly changing marketplace environment in which we work. The good and great in advertising are probably differentiated by how fast they are able to catch up with the changes.

Where there's a will, there's a solution to any given challenge.

HAVE FUN AND ENJOY EVERY MOMENT

You will grow old and die very quickly in this industry if you don't seize the moments worth enjoying—and there are plenty in advertising. They give you the energy to face the battle the next day, even after a devastating defeat at work.

Follow this rule and you will probably keep younger than your peers. Come to think of it, this could well be an idea for our next skin care advertising!

This veteran also said to me, "Do your work well and great things will happen naturally!" I wish you success in advertising.

JIMMY LIANG

Friends of Jörg

Operations Director,
Leo Burnett Advertising, Shanghai, China

Jimmy was born in Beijing. He and his family moved to Hong Kong in the early 70s.

A graduate of the Chinese University of Hong Kong, Jimmy started his career—while at college—as an intern for a year with Ogilvy & Mather Direct on the American Express Card card. After graduation, he continued to work at Ogilvy, and subsequently at Young & Rubicam, DDB and Bates Advertising / 141 Marketing Communication.

Taking advantage of his linguistic ability in Mandarin, Jimmy established his business network on the Greater China concept in 1995. He has been mainly responsible for the PRC with his practical, on-the-ground work experience managing FMCGs, the media and consumer technology brands / clients. His experience includes marketing and sales in the areas of regional satellite TV and cable, the Internet, event marketing, and print publishing.

In the last 10 years, Jimmy has spent more than half of his time commuting, working and living in Shanghai, Guangzhou and Beijing.

He has managed all the Wrigley China brands (chewing gum and confectionery) whose target groups range from kids (brand Tata) and teens (brand Juicy Fruit) to urban white collars (brand Extra) and the general public (brand Doublemint) since he joined Leo Burnett Guangzhou as Business Director in early 2005. He was lately promoted to the position of Operations Director to manage the day-to-day operations of the LB GZ office.

In 2006, Jimmy was selected as one of the 22 agency innovators worldwide by *inter-national-ist* magazine (www.inter-national-ist.com) for the unconventional communication ideas and approaches he has helped his clients plan and execute in the rapidly changing market environment.

Audi
The new Audi TT Coupé.
The wait is almost over.
You've coveted the Audi TT for long enough, so book now to secure one of the few left available and avoid waiting any longer than you'd really have to.
For more information, visit the Audi TT Lounge at www.audi.com.sg and gain fascinating insights into the styling and technology of the Audi TT Coupé's iconic design.
Premium Automobiles 199902271W
Showrooms: 9 Leng Kee Road Singapore 159090 Tel: 6566 1111 • 55 Ubi Road 1 Singapore 408699 Tel: 6388 2323

Vorsprung durch Technik www.audi.com.sg
Audi
The new Audi TT Coupé.
The wait is almost over.
Now yours to own with a special pre-launch offer, for a limited time only.
For more information, visit the Audi TT Lounge at www.audi.com.sg and gain fascinating insights into the styling and technology of the Audi TT Coupé's iconic design.
Premium Automobiles 199902271W

Vorsprung durch Technik www.audi.com.sg
Audi
TT
The new Audi TT Coupé.
The wait is almost over.
Now yours to own with a special pre-launch offer, for a limited time only.
For more information, visit the Audi TT Lounge at www.audi.com.sg and gain fascinating insights into the styling and technology of the Audi TT Coupe's iconic design.
TÜV
Premium Automobiles 199902271W
Showrooms: 9 Leng Kee Road Singapore 159090 Tel: 6566 1111 • 55 Ubi Road 1 Singapore 408699 Tel: 6388 2323

Vorsprung durch Technik www.audi.com.sg
HH PK 156
The new Audi TT Coupé.
Pure energy.
A new dawn of power has arrived. Eight years after the introduction of the iconic original, the new Audi TT Cou
is as uncompromising a sports car as ever – charged with refined energy in every detail.
Explosive dynamism on the road is generated by either the 2.0 TFSI or the 3.2 V6 quattro® engine wrapped in t
new ASF® Audi Space Frame – where the strength of steel is infused with aluminium's lightness. Now, respons
handling, forceful acceleration and fuel economy are all embodied within a single form.
The new Audi TT Coupé. Pure energy – with the power to electrify.
Premium Automobiles 199902271W
Showrooms: 9 Leng Kee Road Singapore 159090 Tel: 6566 1111 • 55 Ubi Road 1 Singapore 408699 Tel: 6388 2

Audi

CAMPAIGN TITLE
AUDI TT

CLIENT
Audi Premium Automobiles

AGENCY
formul8 Singapore

AGENCY CREDITS
Rustam Muhammad – Creative Director
Clinton Low – Art Director
Edwin Leong – Copywriter
Harish Nambiar – Account Servicing

TIME FRAME OF CAMPAIGN
3 months running up to the launch of the Audi TT

CAMPAIGN TITLE
Audi TT

OBJECTIVES OF CAMPAIGN
To create a teaser campaign to create interest and drive sales for the new Audi TT, and subsequently launch the Audi TT

TARGET GROUP
Dynamic and upwardly mobile PMEBs aged between 30 and 45, as well as 'autophiles'.

PROPOSITION
- Every iteration of the Audi TT embodies clean design, coupled with sheer performance and driving pleasure
- Something that's especially true for the latest incarnation of the iconic TT.

COMMUNICATION STRATEGY
The teaser campaign was that the wait for the newly redesigned Audi TT, first introduced eight years ago, was well worth it. Following this, the launch ad would then reveal the new lines, pure power and dynamism of the new Audi TT.

CHOICE OF MEDIA

Above-The-Line: *Straits Times, Business Times, The Edge, Peak*
Below-The-Line: Invite / Poster

CREATIVE EXECUTION

A series of visuals with the silver-silhouetted car serves to accentuate the fluid lines that make the Audi TT an icon among automobiles, while creating a sense of mystique hinting at things to come. While evocative of the original, the new model features an even sleeker, curvier and more imposing presence. The headline, naturally, plays on the eight years both Audi and motoring enthusiasts have had to wait for its arrival. At long last, their wait for a car that reinvented the look and drive of the sports coupé is almost over.

This approach neatly segues into the execution for the launch advertisement where the visual features the Audi TT speeding down a lit tunnel. This serves not only to shed some light on the new TT but also accentuates its features of pure power and dynamism; the detail of the tunnel lighting up as it approaches further extends the theme of pure energy in the headline.

COUNTRIES COVERED

Singapore

RESULTS

Premium Automobiles, the Singapore Audi distributor, has more than exceeded its 2006 sales targets for the model.

8. What you need vs What you want

These days, with so many media options for you to choose from, it is hard to make the right decision without some criteria. Basically, before we discuss the strengths and weaknesses of the different types of advertising media, here are some basics:

1. Choose the medium that is best suited to get your message across. You may want to create an emotional tie-in with your brand. Using TV and radio allows you to address the different senses and interact emotionally with your target group. It will give you a better opportunity to get emotions across to your target than if you use, say, an Internet banner.

2. Choose the medium that you know will reach your target group. Know what their day looks like and what their media consumption habits are.

A combination of the two criteria will help you to reach a decision on some of the choices that are right for the particular message that you want to convey and the particular target group you want to reach. This is often easier said than done. You need the help of a good media planner to determine which medium is best.

MEDIA PLANNING

A good media planner would have an in-depth understanding of your target. Together, you would look at a typical day in the target group's life. Let's take myself, for example:

A day in the life ... (an obscure Beatles reference that works if you're a fan or over 40, but it's ok, it'll work without decoding, too)

06.30	Wake up	By radio alarm, but too short a time to listen to any ad messages because I don't want to wake up the whole household.
07.00	Breakfast	I read the *International Herald Tribune*—and look at the ads there. (**press ads**)
07.20	Drive to work	I listen to the radio in the car: First BBC World until 7.35, then Power 98 (including the **radio ads**). I pass some billboards on the way to work and may overtake some taxis and buses—so, I'd see some **outdoor ads**.

07.45	Start work	I am constantly online when I am in the office and checking my work mail, school mail and online mail. I also visit different websites and read some blogs. In this way, I am exposed to **online ads**.
12.30	Lunch	Most of the time I eat on campus; sometimes I have business luncheons in restaurants and this gives me more exposure to **outdoor ads.**
14.00	Back to work	I may teach a class. Students always tell me about new campaigns or products that they have seen. (**word of mouth**). Or sometimes, I may take a flight to a meeting in HK. On my frequent trips I am exposed to **magazine ads**, **inflight TV ads**, **outdoor ads** at the airport, **billboards** on the way from the airport to the hotel, CNN in my hotel room (**TV ads**) and the excellent *South China Morning Post* (**press ads**).
19.00	End work	If I am not travelling, I may go to the gym (**outdoor ads** on the way) or do some shopping (**Point of Sale** at the stores).
21.00	Home	I see some billboards (**outdoor ads**) on the way home, listen to the radio in the car (**radio ads**), read my mail when I get home (**Direct Mail**), then watch some TV (**TV ads**), check my email once more (**online ads**), walk the dogs (potentially outdoor, but ours is a quiet neighbourhood), then go to sleep.

You see, if you know your target group inside out and what their lives and days look like, the media planner can give you an idea about

- which media to use and
- within a specific medium, which title, station or programme to focus on.

Don't forget that within the communication mix, you have more tools than just advertising. You can also use PR, online and the many tools under Sales Promotion.

Your media planner will put together a media plan which will not only list the different channels you should use to reach your target, but also how often your ad should run to reach a specified frequency. Research has shown that consumers have to be shown an ad at least three or four times to make sure they will remember it. We call this frequency. A good media plan will give you a frequency of five times or so with a certain percentage or reach of your specified target. Some advertisers believe more is better and bombard customers with the same commercial over and over again. Interestingly, research has shown that there is no specific number after which the ad becomes counterproductive and consumers start to get annoyed. It very much depends on the ad and how well it is made. Bad ads become annoying very quickly but, unfortunately, these are often the ones with the big media budget for overexposure. In the meantime, great ads, which are shown maybe in different cuts to add some variety, can run for a long time before consumers switch off. The media plan will suggest whether to keep a continuous presence in one medium or whether to advertise in waves.

MEDIA BUYING

Once you have approved the media plan, the media buyer will start to book your ads in the media selected, at pre-negotiated rates: And, the more you spend, the better the rate you will get. Media rates are extremely flexible. Nobody pays the official price quoted on the rate card of the chosen media. (That's why official figures on the media spend of competitors must be taken with a pinch of salt. They are always based on the official 'rate card' price, when, in reality, the advertiser may have enjoyed discounts of up to 40%.)

Before we look at the different media and their strengths and weaknesses, let's look at another tool that is becoming more important recently.

PR

Public Relations, or Publicity, is part of the Integrated Marketing Communications mix even though, in reality, it is often divorced from advertising. On the client side, the two disciplines may be looked after by different departments and, on the agency side, by different specialised

DAVID GUERRERO

Friends of Jörg

Chairman,
Chief Creative Officer,
BBDO Guerrero Ortega, Philippines

Hi. My name's David Guerrero. I'm a Filipino who grew up in England. So my first working experiences were in London. However I never forgot where I was from. An early radio commercial I made even featured Imelda and her shoes. I then spent five years working in Hong Kong.

Please give us three examples of your work which you love so much or which people highly praise.

VISA 'DINING OUT'

Hong Kong influenced me in many ways—particularly in the launch of the new Asia Pacific campaign for VISA entitled 'All it takes.' This campaign has been running in the region since 2001. In this spot, someone eating in a restaurant finds the soup 'too salty.' She then has an argument with the cook and waiters and destroys the restaurant she's in—settling the bill with her card. We were lucky enough to cast Zhang Ziyi, who had just made *Crouching Tiger, Hidden Dragon*—and at the time could barely speak English. The spot was ranked in the world's top 20 by the Gunn Report the following year.

FHM 'BIG WORDS'

The next ad—for the Philippines *FHM* magazine—was featured by Ad Age as 'one of the 10 ads America won't be seeing' in the year we did it. It's based on a simple insight that the people who buy *FHM* are not really looking at the articles as much as the pictures of near-naked women. Our local client loved it. But the international owners ultimately asked us to withdraw the ad from advertising award shows because they felt it would damage their standing with US advertisers!

WWF ' PETITION'

We're very proud of this 2006 piece of work. With global warming being the leading international issue, we thought that a petition to ask local lawmakers to pass a law in favour of renewable energy sources could directly spell out the benefits. With every person that signs, the ink in the pen goes down.

Q & A

Q: What are the times that make you really feel "I've got the best job on earth"? Or when you felt like... "I'm going to give this up." How do you deal with this feeling?

A: Coming up with a good idea. Getting a good idea killed by a client. I then realise that we obviously haven't done enough to draw the connection in the client's mind between great work and great business results. And I resolve to do more to help them see that. Of course if that doesn't work, it's quite possible we have the wrong client. There are many, many clients in the world and it's simply not possible to get on with all of them.

Q: What got you started in advertising?

A: The chance to change people's minds. And the realisation in 1980s Britain, when I was growing up, that advertising could be used to sell ideas as much as products. Of course many people have realised that already. I recently saw a documentary on John Lennon and, even in the 60s, he saw peace as a product like any other that people had become familiar with.

Q: For you, where do good ideas come from?

A: From inner space—they spring out of deep personal convictions about how the world works and what is right. That and a lot of information, knowledge and understanding—you can't create good ideas in a vacuum.

Q: Commercial work is for brands and consumers yet they reflect the characteristics, philosophy or feelings of the creative people responsible for delivering the executions. Is this very true for you? If so, is this a natural reflection or more than that: Are you the force?

A: Great work has to come from an individual with an individual in mind. I believe that you need to feel a real conviction about what you're doing to communicate successfully. However, I think any idea of individuality about creating advertising must be tempered with the fact that we are at the mercy of the market. And of what works with the people we're talking to. That's the difference between us and pure visual artists for example. In the case of artists, we expect them to be true to their personal vision regardless of whether anyone else likes it or not. In the case of advertising creatives, the genius lies in the ability to carry a defined audience along with them. Sometimes that audience is quite small—it might even be, in some cases, an audience consisting entirely of award show judges! But if they fail to convince the people they are talking to, they have failed.

Q: Are there any TV spots or campaigns that you're giving super attention to? Or wished they were yours? Or anyone creative that you're checking out lately? Or is there anything that attracts you that is NOT advertising?

A: There is work that I respond to genuinely as a consumer. Although living in the Philippines, I don't only see what runs in our market. One of the great branding ideas which I was recruited into early was the nikeplus concept. As a runner, and someone who loves music, the bringing together of these premium brands in one community site was definitely something that impressed me. Although funnily enough I'm not envious of the people who did it. I'm just glad that they did!

In terms of things that aren't advertising, I'm most attracted by fictional writing, that includes authors such as Ian McKewan, Ali Smith, Dave Eggers and Neal Stephenson. The Simpsons, Ricky Gervais, and Monty Python make me laugh. And I enjoy the portrayals of Asia in the movies of Quentin Tarantino, Wong Kar Wai, Sophia Coppola, Zhang Yi Mou and, obviously, Ang Lee.

Q: How do you think advertising will change in the future?

A: Advertising will have to make a significantly positive impact in its community or it will ultimately be ignored, or banned. The Sao Paolo clean-up of the city's billboards—where the city ordered all of them to be dismantled—is a real wake-up call for the industry. Or should be. More positively, we're seeing some of the most awarded work doing something good for the community. One example is the South African bank which created a billboard that also provided free solar powered electricity for a local school. The idea brought the brand promise to life—and was recognised with the Grand Prix at Cannes.

Q: What is the most important thing in your life?

A: Being true to myself. My personal values are to promote excellence in creativity, to reward people for their efforts, to play my own small part in the continuing development of our country and, of course, to do my best for our two children.

David was ranked as one of Asia's Top 10 Creatives by Campaign Brief Asia and was only one of three people to have been inducted into the Philippine Creative Guild Hall of Fame. He is head of BBDO Asia Pacific Creative Council and Regional Creative Director for FedEx. David also headed the Radio Lions Jury at the 2007 Cannes International Advertising Festival.

companies. Some agencies may offer an all-in, 360-degree approach, but often that is more wishful thinking than reality.

The PR sector is booming these days because of the change in consumer behaviour. The arrival of the new, better informed, 'emancipated' and empowered consumers has led to a decrease in the power of advertising. Consumers don't have to rely on advertising messages any more for information; instead they can do a simple online search and find the information they want both from the manufacturer as well as from trusted sources like blogs that share personal blogger experiences with the brand. Also, consumers have seen many an over-promise in the past and have become more skeptical, some even cynical, about advertising messages: "Of course they would say that. They want to sell their product. But that doesn't mean it's true."

Trust in advertising is still greater in countries like China where consumers know that there are very strict government guidelines about what can be claimed in an ad and what can't. But, overall, the new consumer has become a skeptic, worldwide.

There are several way to generate publicity:

- issue a press release about a new brand or product or an improvement;
- hold a press conference where the CEO engages the press;
- give product samples to the press and encourage them to test the product;
- sponsor an event;
- use a celebrity spokesperson (see risks outlined in an earlier chapter).

In general, consumers tend to believe press or TV reports from reputable media more since they know that the medium's own reputation rests on the assumption that their reporting is free and fair. The newspaper, website or TV channel acts as a filter that will pass through only messages that are proven to be true and that are tried and tested.

But there is a lot of competition in these channels and space is limited. Moreover, you will have little control as to exactly what will be reported, when the report will be out and what percentage of your target group will read or see it. You will need to build a good relationship with the relevant journalists that cover your industry, e.g. by buying them lunch, inviting them to product launches, test-drives or dinners.

Journalists appreciate it if you make their lives easy by:

- writing a press release from their point of view which they can use without rewriting if they want to;
- providing them with 'editorial' pictures instead of 'beauty shots' as that will make the report more interesting;
- providing them with rare and raw TV footage that they can edit and use for their article;
- feeding them once in a while because they don't get paid so much.

There is a fine line between relationship-building and bribing. Tread this cautiously. It differs from market to market. In developing countries like China, there may be an expectation for you to 'give more'. How far you want to go depends on your personal values and company policy. Just be aware of the fact that attempts at bribing can often backfire, either when the bribe is refused (and the relationship thus turns sour) or when the public finds out and subsequently turns against your brand.

THE LINE

You may hear advertising practitioners talk about an ABOVE-THE-LINE (ATL) or BELOW-THE-LINE (BTL) campaign. I have no idea where that line comes from. If you do, drop me a mail. This has been confusing for many of my students. To my test question, "What is the difference between above-the-line and below-the-line?", they give answers such as, "Depends on how thick the line is," or "Below-the-line is when you make fun of people, like because they are fat." Uhm, no. That's not below-the-line. That's below the belt.

It is merely a distinction that has been used to distinguish between media that talk:

(a) ONE to MANY. Where one manufacturer talks to many customers at the same time, as in TV, cinema, radio, outdoor, print and press (ATL).
(b) ONE to ONE. As in direct marketing, mailers and brochures (BTL).

The distinction is no longer relevant because there are now mass media like print that have become more tailored and may include response elements such as coupons, phone numbers or websites that turn the relationship from one-to-many into one-to-one.

It is also unclear where we would place online ads. Some online ads and websites aim at a mass audience, but at the same time, deliver tailored messages.

360

Besides above-the-line and below-the-line, you may sometimes hear of a 'through-the-line' campaign. This describes a truly integrated marketing communications campaign that uses many of the tools and channels, both with a mass and personal appeal. In fact, I would argue that most campaigns these days are through-the-line, trying to cut through the clutter to get the message across in many different ways and hoping that 'the best swimmer' will reach the intended audience.

Integration is the buzzword, and marketers are using different media to not just increase their chances of reaching their target, but also to tailor their messages by using the strengths of different media, e.g. TV for emotional bonding, press for quick reaction, DM for personalised offers and online for offering depth of information.

Agencies which used to be only ATL or BTL now offer an integrated approach, famously named '360 degrees brand stewardship' by Ogilvy, and shortened to '360' in today's market speak. The idea makes sense in theory, but the problem often lies in the execution because:

- agencies have a history. They may have been an ATL agency before, and this will always remain their bias and strength.
- some media are more likely to impress clients (and juries) and thus win awards. This results in a a creative bias towards TVCs and print.
- agencies seldom offer all departments within the same unit. Usually, they are different units 'under one roof' which often leads to rivalry and jealousy, and communications suffers.
- not all agencies have a shared bottom line for their departments, so every department fights for its own ideas without looking at the bigger picture.

The client has also a responsibility to make sure that there is seamless teamwork right from the start. He should direct the ad agency to work closely with the PR agency and media agency so that the proposal that is presented to him is a combined effort of all three parties.

I used to travel regionally to attend local presentations by both our creative and media agencies where creative presented work that found no expression in the media plan, and where the media agency presented some creative ideas and layouts of their own to provide the content for some of the media they had chosen. The end result was that the local clients would look from one to the other, shake their heads and ask, "Do you guys ever TALK to each other?"

9. Various media

There are many channels to get your message across, to connect with consumers. We will have a look at their strengths and weaknesses.

PRINT

For press, the big advantages are that it has a fast turnaround, high coverage and is a relatively trusted medium. It is not big on emotion, but if you have to urgently address your target or the general population to reassure them, e.g. that your product is safe after some bad press reports, you can book an ad today and see it in the press tomorrow, space permitting.

It may be argued that, for this example, PR may be a better avenue as people find the message more credible since a (supposedly neutral) third-party issues the statement and not the brand owner/manufacturer himself. But with PR, you also have no absolute control since independent journalists will express their own views and experiences that may or may not be positive for your brand. That's why with PR, you may want to complement your press release or conference with a full page 'Letter from the Chairman' to make sure your message is understood. It's also a medium that can be very targeted, depending on what newspaper you choose and where in the newspaper you place your ad. You may be tempted to go 'big' and book a double-page-spread (DPS) but sometimes it may be better to place a single page ad next to editorial content, where people spend more time reading, and the page stays open longer. But keep in mind that printing press quality may vary across regional newspapers, so a subtle black to grey gradient background with small white print may turn into a black hole, e.g. in Indonesia or India.

Magazines are good to target specific customer groups. People spend more time reading them and there is a loyal readership. Magazines also have a longer shelf life—well beyond their publication dates so that you have more people seeing your ad. Don't you wish the one issue with your ad ended up in your doctor's waiting room? Make sure you choose magazines mostly for rational-based advertising and construct ads with some information, not just pure image. Printing quality is usually very good, so you can add emotion by using colourful pictures. New formats are constantly developing—you can now add a fragrance to your ad, increase the size by booking a fold-out or direct the reader to your ad by putting a bookmark. Your media planner should know which magazines offer special formats. One disadvantage is that magazines have a very long lead time of up to one month as most of them are published monthly, so your ad needs to be ready to print four weeks before the start of the campaign.

RADIO

By now we know that video did not kill the radio star, and that this medium is more resilient than we thought. Radio listening has changed a bit, from being the sole family information and entertainment medium before the arrival of TV to being the medium 'on the go'. There are advantages in this too, and these days radio is most often used for more tactical advertising such as to persuade consumers to stop for petrol or to go to the supermarket; or to create traffic for some local, time-dependent promotion. Radio allows you to deliver your ad to a targeted group by identifying the right station and time of day; reach busy and elusive business people; and can be very localized, supporting your point-of-sale promotional activities. It works very immediately, driving traffic and generating trial instead of long-term brand building. Some creatives think that just relying on audio can be very limiting, but great radio campaigns have proven them wrong, like 'Great Men of Genius' by Bud Light in the US.

OUTDOOR

With more media and more messages out to reach consumers, it has become harder to cut through the clutter. But whatever people do, even if they don't spend money on magazines and never switch on their TV, they will eventually have to leave the house to go for a meal or buy some groceries. That's when they cannot escape outdoor or out-of-home (OOH) advertising from billboards to bus-stands, ads on the roofs of taxis, on buses, in underground stations and trains. With OOH, you only have a few seconds to grab the attention of your target. Sometimes, the consumer may see your billboard from a distance, so keep your message short and simple. Shrink it and place it on a matchbox. If it still works, it will work as a billboard.

Advertising out of home has in fact become so ubiquitous that consumers have developed a skill for tuning them out, unless you are using a special format like wrapping up the IFC2 tower in Hong Kong, having football players play on a vertical pitch above the roofs of Tokyo, building a whole zoo on top of a bus station, putting IWC-watches on bus handlebars or placing some real plane tires in an underground train station, as DHL in Hong Kong has. For outdoor ads, there is no limit to the creative use of space, and it normally leaves open options available for the agency to negotiate with the media owner and local authorities to get a new format approved. Recent years have seen an upsurge in creative outdoor ads, with many award-winning and impactful new ideas from Asia and beyond. Outdoor advertising is quite general in its targeting, although some billboards can be booked individually to reach, say, business travellers on their way to the airport.

The production process for print media and outdoor advertising is quite similar:

- the creative team comes up with a layout of headline, body copy and visual
- client approves the ad (plus legal checks, if necessary)
- print production hires photographer, if necessary, or buys stock footage
- photographer/production casts talent (models) if necessary
- photographer shoots visuals (sometimes re-shooting can be cheaper than stock footage)
- post-production takes place, combining images and words
- client gives final approval
- materials are produced

TV

For many, creatives and clients alike, shooting a TV Commercial (TVC) is still the 'holy grail' of advertising. TVCs can be funny and emotional; they can be touching and shocking. Ideally, they should tell a story or express an attitude. They can create the emotional value of a brand and position it, and appeal to the hearts and minds of consumers. By using sound, dialogue, music and visuals, they can achieve an overall effect that is more powerful than most other media if there is a captive and appreciative audience.

Most TVCs are shot on film and then cut down to 45 or 30 seconds, the most used format around the world. Sometimes,15-second cut-down versions are produced because it is the locally prevalent format, as is the case in Japan or Korea, where only 15-second TVCs are allowed. In this case, the director would use a different cut because the shorter version may not be effective, as it cannot be assumed that the audience knows the story.

Longer versions of 60 and 90 seconds are sometimes used in cinemas.

With TV still being the most impactful medium, many creatives have a TV bias and try to push ideas towards TVC executions, aiming at visibility for the agency, peer recognition and awards. Unfortunately, many clients play along and agree to shoot a TVC even though it may not be the best medium to reach their target or to make the most out of their limited budget.

The production of a TV commercial is more complicated than a print ad and follows, in general terms, these steps:

- The creative team develops a TV script, in written form (script/treatment).
- The client approves the idea and informs the agency of his production budget.
- The agency draws up the key scenes of the TVC (storyboard).
- Sometimes, the storyboard gets tested with consumers.
- The TV production department receives the director brief from the creative team.
- TV production looks for suitable directors (based on the show reel of their previous work) and determines whether they like the script, whether they are available and whether their cost is within the given budget.
- Agency presents three directors to the client, with one as agency recommendation, and a rough indication of timing and cost.
- Client approves choice of director.
- Director comes with a production company. Most directors work with the same company all the time and sometimes, they may own them.
- Production company delivers a detailed estimate, including possible bad-weather-insurance and talent or music royalties for use of talent over time and in specific locations.
- Agency and client determine who needs to attend the shoot; diaries are blocked and travel arrangements are made.
- Director delivers a shooting board, i.e. a storyboard with his interpretation of the key scenes.
- Production company sends location scouts to source a location. If it isn't a recognisable location, the production company will make use of local knowledge and connections.
- Client approves location.
- Director or production company brief casting agency to start casting and recommend talent to the agency which recommends to the client and gets his feedback/approval.
- In a Pre-Preproduction Meeting (pre-PPM), client, agency, (agency's) TV producer and (director's) production company discuss the shooting-board,

location, talent, props and styling (of location and people).

- Everybody travels to the shooting location; final PPM.
- Shoot (depending on the story, two or three days).
- Post-production is normally conducted in a separate location which has the facilities and lower cost, such as Hong Kong or Bangkok. This process includes editing, colour grading, music, supers and voice-over.
- The almost finished TVC is presented to client for final approval (offline) before final fine-tuning.
- Station-copies are made and sent out.

Timing and price for the production of a TV commercial vary depending on the budget and the client's time constraints. Overall production time can go from six weeks to six months and costs can range from US$50,000 to over $1 million.

ONLINE

The Internet has changed everybody's lives. For many target groups such as students, it has become the No 1 medium for information and entertainment. The students in my classes in Singapore are online 85% of their waking hours, whether they are at school, at home and/or at cafes and hotspots. Companies need to have a strong Internet-presence, given its prevalence as the first place where people look for information today. If your company is not there, it does not exist or cannot be trusted. If your website is boring, slow or outdated, so is your brand. Some have argued that the mere presence on the web is advertising for your brand. This is true to a certain extent since, unlike the Yellow Pages, the Internet does not just list your company. Instead, you can decide how you want to portray your brand, by choosing colours, typeface, animation, flash, games etc. So the way you construct your Internet presence is another touch point which helps to position your brand. Just make sure your presence is constructed by an expert, so your Internet website does not only work well and load fast, but also comes up first in a Google-search about your segment or industry.

There is your company presence on the Internet, but there are many other ways to advertise in the cyber world. These can include banners, sponsored searches on Google, Yahoo-ads, and annoying pop-ups. There are also consumer blogs and viral marketing.

TERM SHON

Friends of Jörg

Professor, Visual Communications,
Hansei University,
Seoul, Korea

Advertising In Korea

Consumer behaviour in Korea is similar to that in Japan—based on the fact that Japan was Asia's first economic power. It set the example for Koreans. Korean consumers are more straightforward in their attitudes and behaviour, as compared to Europeans. All that counts is 'The Brand'. Everything that is expensive must be good and has to be bought.

For example: A new beauty product was introduced to the market. The introductory price was low—big mistake. Consumers did not bite, thinking a cheap product must be bad. They did not want to be seen using it. It bombed. A short while later, the same manufacturer introduced a new product. It was expensive. And it was a big success...

Cheap products hardly have a chance to survive in the Korean market. It's all about brands—that's why most fake brands are found in Asia. Demand is quicker than supply. Which means that there is no time to produce great advertising. No Cannes quality here. Whether a Korean agency develops creative advertising isn't important in this country's business world.

Korea is a country of hungry consumers, always on the hunt for the latest statement.

Professor Term Shon has worked in advertising agencies in Korea and Germany as an award-winning Art Director, looking after clients like Volkswagen, Kumho tyres, Samsung and Lotte. Since 2006, he has been teaching visual communication at Seoul's Hansei University. He works in Seoul and Berlin.

Viral marketing is an interesting tool which uses the voluntary co-operation of Internet users to spread your brand message. It is all about creating a small ad, a game or a video which can be downloaded from your website. Alternatively, you yourself can start the ball rolling by sending it out via email. Most of the time, because its content is unique, interesting or funny, these viral games or videos will be emailed from friend to friend as a matter of interest. To succeed at this, your online agency needs to be very tuned in to the likes and dislikes of your target group in order to create an ad that they like and find email-worthy. If it works, you would have created a lot of buzz, interest and goodwill for your brand at a relatively low cost.

BLOGGING

Blogging is an Internet phenomenon, where customers use their own website or specific blog-sites to create an online diary (from web-log) to share their experiences and thoughts. There are millions of blogs out there, and many of them go unnoticed by everybody but the blogger and his friends. But some, because they write well and are funny or because they are famous or controversial, command a big following who wait for every new instalment. Most of these bloggers are fiercely independent and sometimes anti-consumerist. They hold a certain skepticism towards big business and also big government. Some test products or brands in their blogs and share their findings with their readership. What makes blogs special is that most of them are written without an ad agency. They are seen to represent the genuine opinion of their writers and have therefore a high credibility amongst the readers.

Modern consumers are driven by any of these factors when they look for a new product:

- they have run out of it or their current product is broken, faulty or old
- their current product is still working but missing many of the functions that the new product offers
- nothing is wrong with their current product and the life cycle has not reached its end, but advertisers have created a new need in their minds and hearts
- all their friends have the latest version and they do not want to be left behind

So when they are in the market for a new product, they first look for information:

- in their own memory. (What was it like the last time they bought a product? And were they happy with the brand they used?)
- online. (What does the manufacturer site say about the latest offer? What do independent sites say about comparisons? What do consumers (bloggers) say about this new product/brand?)

After they have narrowed down the relevant set to a more manageable number of products and brands, consumers compare features, designs and prices. They may go to the shop or showroom to experience the brand with their senses before making a decision to purchase. After the purchase, they will evaluate their decision to see if it is the correct one. That's why advertising has not only to ensure that the brand appears in the information search and that the review/feedback the consumers read is positive, but also to reassure consumers after they've made a purchase that their decision is right. In some cases, communication after the purchase can help to post-rationalise an emotional decision, as for example, the case with men for cars.

Marketers can use blogs as an important source of information about what (some) consumers think about their products and brands, or as an early-warning system in case there is something negative about their brand. However, you should always keep in mind that bloggers are the influential few, and their opinion may not necessarily be the opinion of the majority.

When a blogger sends out a bad review about a product or service, there is often a temptation to react. Most of the time, that is not a good idea as the blogger will view the given explanation with cynicism. Instead of engaging directly with the blogger, it is better to let the review pass or use PR to make a point. Clients should never try to bully the blogger or attempt to buy him off. That will only backfire and hurt the brand.

Can companies use the blogging phenomenon to their advantage? Well, some bloggers, like journalists, are prepared to accept a product in order to test it, if it's a no-strings-sampling process. If you believe in your product and have reason to believe that they will conduct a fair test (judging from their earlier postings), then by all means give them your new product and hope for the best. Some CEOs have taken to blogging—but I am not sure if consumers are attracted to their sites, knowing that these sites will not be completely objective. Don't put up an 'independent' blog that pushes your brand—companies have tried (often with the help of their PR agencies) and failed. The backlash, once you are found out, is much worse than the potential goodwill you can create. It's not worth the risk.

GUERRILLA

Some agencies specialise in guerrilla marketing—a new, unorthodox way of getting your product and brand noticed and of making a point about the competition. The background to this is that some brands have positioned themselves as quirky and rebellious, and it supports their positioning to use different ways of communication. Another is that many consumers have become numb towards conventional messages and channels, so guerrilla marketing is the only way to get through to them. For certain target groups, namely teenagers and young adults, guerrilla marketing has the highest street credibility since it ties in with their own rebel-image.

Ogilvy Red Card has done some great work in this field. This includes dressing a Ronald McDonald figure in an 'I love Burger King' T-Shirt. But the impact is often limited since many guerrilla campaigns walk on the fringes of the law. Sometimes, they may be outright illegal, and so, not many people have the chance to see them. Big brands often shy away from using guerrilla tactics because of the fear of legal problems that can hurt their reputation.

DIRECT MARKETING

In a time when consumers are looking for more tailored messages and offers, direct marketing is an important tool to speak to them one-on-one. A direct mailer for a Victoria's Secret catalogue, an invitation to view a condominium or to test-drive an Audi can be easily personalised and is thus likely to attract the recipient's attention. You may have received *The Economist*'s famous, award-winning direct mailer in the form of an internal company envelope which had the names of Bill Clinton and Kofi Annan crossed out, followed by the uncrossed name of the recipient. Of course we must all have realised that it was mass-personalised, but it was a flattering idea and it made us smile. Perhaps it even made us subscribe to *The Economist*. Some direct mailers work with the knowledge that many people feel the need to reciprocate when they are given a present so they include pens or personalised name-stickers with the letter asking for a charity donation.

SALES PROMOTION

With consumers becoming harder to reach in a crowded market of competing products and brands, Sales Promotions is an area that has been growing in recent years. There are dozens of tools for Sales Promotions, but here are some of the most common ones:

SALES PROMOTION TOOLS

CONSUMER-ORIENTED

- BONUS PACKS
- CONTESTS/SWEEPSTAKES
- COUPONS
- EVENT MARKETING
- FREQUENCY PROGRAMMES
- PREMIUMS
- PRICE-OFF DEALS
- PRICE-PACK DEALS
- REFUNDS/REBATES
- SAMPLES

TRADE-ORIENTED

- CONTESTS, DEALER INCENTIVES
- COOPERATIVE ADVERTISING
- LISTING FEES
- POINT-OF-PURCHASE DISPLAYS
- TRADE ALLOWANCES
- TRAINING PROGRAMMES
- TRADE SHOWS

LOYALTY SCHEMES

Some of these schemes are aimed at increasing customer loyalty. That, in itself, is not a difficult job. If you have a great brand, customers will want to be loyal and they will buy your brand in all its expressions, even without any reward or discount. But for brands that are commodities or where the differences are smaller, particularly in the area of travel (hotels, airlines, rental cars), loyalty schemes have worked remarkably well. The downside is that travellers have collected so many airline miles through frequent flyer programmes or tie-ups with partners such as credit card companies, that airlines are now hard pressed to release enough seats for mileage-redemption-trips to avoid customer frustration and complaints. After all, airlines would rather sell the seats, if they could, rather than give them away for free. Intelligent systems, however, often target not just the brand or service user but also the influencer: I'll never forget that Heike, my secretary in London, once had a free weekend in Paris—courtesy of the miles she had collected with British Airways 'Executive Secretary' scheme for trips she had booked for me on BA.

Pretty happy. Haha, pardon the pun. For a celebrity TVC, it's working. And Drizzle was pretty cool, introduced me to some Korean babes. Now Mr. Wang wants to do different language versions. Expansion to new Asian markets. Do they like jelly outside China? Well, I'll put a junior team on it.

FedEx
TAXI

FedEx
Express
fedex.com

'Ambulance'

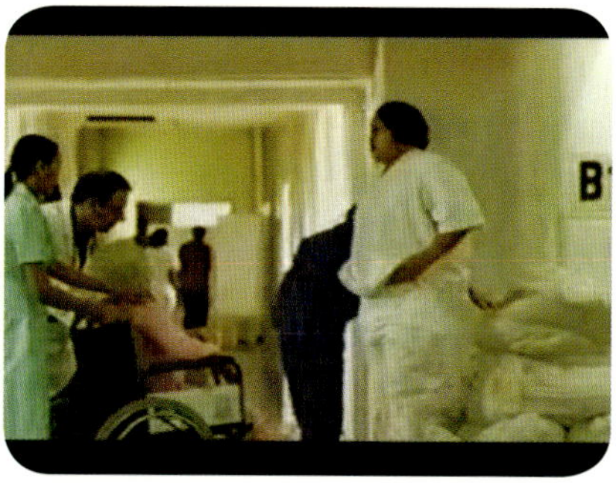

'Difficult Package'

'Jenny'

'Stepping Stones'

CAMPAIGN TITLE
WE LIVE TO DELIVER

CLIENT
FedEx Asia-Pacific

AGENCY
BBDO Asia-Pacific

AGENCY CREDITS
BBDO Guerrero-Ortega (Manila), BBDO Singapore, BBDO Hong Kong

TIME FRAME OF CAMPAIGN
2003 – 2007

CAMPAIGN TITLE
We Live To Deliver

OBJECTIVES OF CAMPAIGN
Establish the 'going above and beyond the call of duty' attitude of the FedEx staff, their dedication and team work which helps them overcome any obstacle.

TARGET GROUP
- Implementors (secretaries, frontline staff who make the final decision about which company to use)
- Generators (C-class management who make the general decision about choosing an express service provider for their company)

PROPOSITION
We live to deliver

COMMUNICATION STRATEGY
- Communicate the attitude
- Show teamwork
- Show examples of the team overcoming obstacles
- Use humour

CHOICE OF MEDIA
Mainly TVCs, supported by print and outdoor.

CREATIVE EXECUTION
Late 1990s – 'Ambulance', 'Pizza'
2003 – 'Jenny'
2004 – 'Pizza'
2005 – 'Stepping Stones'

COUNTRIES COVERED
Asia Pacific

RESULTS
Disproportionately high awareness, Top-Of-Mind (TOM) and 'likely to use' figures

10. Cross-cultural advertising in Asia Pacific

Asia may seem foreign to many marketers if they come from the West and do not understand Asian cultures. The differences in culture, consumer preferences and education are huge. The decisions about brand positioning and communication need to be informed ones, based on a thorough knowledge of the market where the campaign is to be run. One basic fundamental is to be aware of any local taboos.

TABOO AWARENESS

Culture

Some of the restrictions that marketers have to work with are tied to local culture. When FedEx shot its 'Jenny' television commercial in 2003, the local agency, BBDO Bangkok, was shown the storyboard and asked for feedback. The account director reminded the regional agency team, who were based in Hong Kong, that Thais view the showing of the soles of the feet as rude and disrespectful. The storyboard, which featured quite a number of close-up shots of the running feet of 'Jenny', was subsequently amended in order to allow the television commercial to be aired in Thailand.

Nike wasn't so lucky when China banned LeBron James' Nike ad, which saw the star battling dragons and kung fu masters, both of which are highly regarded in the Chinese culture.

Government Policies

Other restrictions may not be inherent in the local culture but may be imposed by the government. In Malaysia, a law requires that all TV advertising must be produced in Malaysia in order to protect the Malaysian film industry and production houses. There are ways around this, for example, by using a talent that looks Malay. However, a marketer has to be aware that he will not be able to 'automatically' show his television commercial in Malaysia.

History

Occasionally, mistakes are made by not taking into account historical factors or sensibilities amongst former enemies like China and Japan. There have been several cases when Japanese ads were banned by Chinese censors who view them as violating China's pride or alluding to the past Japanese occupation.

Other examples include the Toyota's Prado GX and Land Cruiser print ad which offended the Chinese people in 2003. The former showed a pair of stone lions bowing and saluting to the Prado GX on the Marco Polo Bridge while the latter featured the Land Cruiser towing what appeared to be a Chinese military truck. The 2004 Nippon paint ad that showed a dragon sliding down a pillar of a traditional Chinese pavilion painted with Nippon paint was supposed to highlight the smoothness of Nippon paint.

MAXMILLIAN MAK

Friends of Jörg

Group Account Director
TBWA, Hong Kong

Advertising In Hong Kong

As one of Asia's busiest commercial centres and business hubs, Hong Kong certainly is an ideal breeding ground for creative excellence in advertising. Unlike its peers in the Asia Pacific region, Hong Kong has a long history as an independent city and that has enabled its different industries to grow in a more freeform manner. The plus-side of this is that creativity is less bound by the subconscious influence of cultures and heritage, and creative output is as limitless as can be. The other side of the coin, however, is that this freeform growth has bred a mentality of risk-avoidance where everyone over-evaluates everything that can be evaluated, such as effectiveness and awareness. The combined result is a constant see-sawing between wanting to create unprecedented breakthroughs and wanting to reference past performances of such breakthroughs.

With technology enabling a tighter global economy and fading of international boundaries, this situation is quickly changing as keen competition forces marketing and advertising professionals to think out-of-the-box, using tools outside of the usual repertoire. This leads to several changes, with one leading to another.

First is the demand for non-traditional thinking and talents whose expertise lies not so much in creating effective communication with traditional TV and print media, but in other channels such as digital and guerilla tactics.

Secondly, this demand gives rise to smaller shops with a niche in those channels, which in turn pigeon-holes the spectrum of service providers neatly by what they are better at. This change also forces bigger agencies to re-evaluate their service offering and set up divisions and subsidiaries, either organically or through acquisitions, to compete more effectively.

Consequently, marketers have a larger arsenal to plan and execute effective multi-pronged campaigns that reach their customers at different touch-points.

At the same time, they are opening up to exploring new ways of communication where past performance records might not yet be available.

The net result of all these changes is an advertising landscape with a far richer texture than before, shaped by professionals with a deeper understanding of consumers' behaviour and their relationship with the different touch-points who are able to integrate everything under one roof —the brand.

Maxmillian Mak studied in Canada, and graduated from York University with a Bachelor of Arts degree. Upon his return to Hong Kong, he started off his career in advertising at Foote Cone and Belding. Since then, he has worked on both sides of the agency world as a marketer and in account management. His experience covers a diverse range of business categories, ranging from FMCG and retail to consumer and business services. Brands he has worked on include 7-Eleven, Nestle Dairy Farm, Neutrogena, MTR, PCCW, FedEx, VISA and Pizza Hut. As an early believer in the power of integrated marketing communications, he has formed his career around building a comprehensive portfolio in the different areas of marketing, covering advertising, direct marketing, event management, segmentation marketing, and even corporate communication.

But instead, it angered the Chinese people who interpreted the ad as being one that depicted the defeat of the Chinese culture (symbolised by the dragon) to a Japanese product (symbolised by Nippon paint).

Similar sensitivities exist between China and Taiwan. In 2000, China banned advertisements for a Coca-Cola Co. soft drink after the ad's star, Taiwanese singer Sherry Chang Hui-Mei, sang the Taiwanese national anthem to usher in the island's new president.

Being aware of any cultural or historical taboos or sensitivities is just the entry-ticket for communication across markets in Asia. The elimination of potential conflicts may build the foundation for an ad that doesn't offend, but it does not guarantee a credible positioning or local relevance.

The Double Challenge In Asia

There are two primary challenges that marketers in Asia face. First, they need to build a consistent brand across Asian markets. Second, the brand needs to be locally relevant to their target groups in order to stimulate sales, while at the same time minimising funds spent. Faced with this double challenge, marketers are looking for answers to how to communicate effectively in Asia.

BUILDING A CONSISTENT BRAND ACROSS ASIA

Keep To One Common Positioning

It is important for marketers to note that the differences between Asian markets would and should influence decisions they make about the execution of their communication, but not on their brand / product positioning. Consumers in Asia today are highly mobile and quite adept at decoding advertising messages. That, together with a high Internet penetration, which by definition is supranational, establishes the need for a consistent positioning of a product and brand in order to avoid consumer confusion.

While this is true for all brands and products, it is particularly important for premium products, which form the majority of those communicated internationally. These brands sell not so much on functionality but on the desired image they create for the wearer / user. If a consistent image cannot be guaranteed across markets, as with different positioning, the manufacturer loses the price premium since his premium product is now less attractive to consumers.

The Asian positioning should, of course, reflect the market situation in Asia. Let's have a look at FedEx.

At the end of the 90s, FedEx found itself in a challenging position in Asia. DHL was clearly the No 1 international express provider in Asia, having arrived here many years before FedEx and having invested a substantial media spend to build up their positioning. It was widely seen as big and experienced. UPS, on the other hand, had a relatively clear positioning as the express service with the most advanced technology but was a distant third as far as market share was concerned.

FedEx had to find a new positioning in Asia since the market leader positioning that they used in the United States ('Relax, It's FedEx') was not applicable in the Asian environment.

Subsequently, FedEx commissioned a market research company to conduct focus groups in key markets they operated in, to find out what their targets thought about their brand and their competitors' brands.

The advertising agency, BBDO Asia Pacific, then translated these findings into a new core brand value for Asia. The new FedEx promise:

'FedEx. We live to deliver' was born.

This positioning, based on consumer insights in Asia, was also a good match for the company and its philosophy. The tagline was supported by the FedEx philosophy of 'People-Service-Profit'. The message was how FedEx takes extra care of its people who, in turn, will deliver better service to customers and bring in more profit for the company, which would then be re-invested in its people.

So while the new positioning was credible and relevant, it needed to be communicated to the target group across Asia.

FedEx's 'We Live To Deliver' advertising campaign thus rolled out in 1998, focusing on the people who make daily FedEx deliveries possible. Following a pilot campaign series that dramatised FedEx's reliability and capability to deliver packages even under very extreme and difficult situations, there came a number of humour-driven spots. 'Pizza', 'Ambulance', and 'Jenny' were three TVCs that explored the previous lives of today's star FedEx couriers.

Three years later, after each of the regional television commercials had run for a year, another round of focus groups was conducted across Asian markets. The outcome was that consumers found the positioning relevant, original and impactful. The experience and interaction with the actual FedEx employees on a daily basis added credibility to the brand promise.

With a whimsical twist, a later ad campaign in 2004, 'The Difficult Package', showed the ingenuity of an entire FedEx team who needed to deliver an even more challenging parcel. This was the first execution that ran Asia-wide, including China. Subsequent research showed that the commercial was successful in creating top-of-mind awareness in all markets, including China. This was made possible by the fact that, for three years, the consumers in China had been educated about what an express company does and that the new story showed part of the process (pick-up and delivery).

FedEx TV commercials are known worldwide for their creativity and humour. FedEx's TV commercials 'Is It There Yet?' and 'Ambulance' were voted into the 'Top 10 Most Popular TV Commercials' list respectively in the 1997 and 2001 'Most Popular TV Commercial Awards' co-organised annually by Asia Television Limited and The Hong Kong Advertisers Association. 'Difficult Package' was ranked among the top ten most-remembered TV commercials in Singapore in a series of AdTrack surveys collated by MediaCorp TV in 2004 and 2005.

Following that, their next commercial, 'Stepping Stones', and all communication after that, continued along the same premise, staying consistent to the brand positioning. Ironically, the two competitors, DHL and UPS, seem to have realised that this positioning is relevant for the target group: DHL changed its Asian tagline in 2006 to 'All The Way', and UPS now claims to 'Deliver More'.

THE MIDDLE WAY—BEING LOCALLY RELEVANT TO TARGET GROUPS

There is no easy solution or advice to marketers who look at Asia and try to achieve these three: A consistent positioning across all markets, local relevance and minimal spending.

We have already seen that a consistent positioning is imperative and, indeed, possible across all markets in Asia. But the same execution may lack local relevance in some markets. In a number of different studies we looked at consumers in Asia, and the way they receive communication. Some of the lessons learned from this quantitative study were:

Youth Knows No Borders

Young targets are similar across Asia Pacific in the way they look at life, the quest for "there must be something more to life than work", a new confidence and expressiveness. They mostly do as is expected of them but also question the status quo, just like youth everywhere. They value education and material goods, but are also looking for 'more'.

Advertising is a big part of their lives. They grow up seeing ads on TV, online in the cyber world, in magazines, newspapers and at bus stops. They have become 'ad connoisseurs', discussing the latest, coolest ads with their peers and criticising ads that do not live up to their high standards. They appreciate humour in communication and celebrities, especially Asian personalities and not Western imports, are a big part of their lives.

The themes, stars and formats they watch and co-create are similar across the Asia Pacific. A campaign aimed at a younger demographic could probably run in several markets in Asia without many changes if it avoids breaking local taboos.

Markets Can Be Addressed In Groups:

1. The "I am a progressive conservative" Middle Eastern market

These predominantly Muslim countries have an overall conservative culture which is strongly influenced by religion. While this culture influences norms and behaviour, it often does not restrict materialism, the acquisition of material goods and their display, for self-expression. Wealth is good and should be shown.

Any communication in these markets has to take into account the cultural conservatism, the role of men and women and the important status of family. 'Good and clean' advertising that takes on the form of entertainment is most effective.

2. The "I want to get ahead" markets: India, Malaysia, Indonesia, Iran, Vietnam, the Philippines, Thailand and first-tier cities in China

These are the really progressive markets with consumers who see themselves as being on the verge of achieving success. The consumers will work hard to buy the material goods that can express their newfound status and wealth.

The family plays an important role in these still mostly collectivist societies. Achievers are seen ambivalently, with admiration and some disapproval since they break the collective mould. Communication to them is most successful when shown how products and brands can be used to express status and achievement.

3. The "Leading in Asia" markets: Hong Kong, Korea, Taiwan, Singapore

These are probably the most sophisticated markets in Asia where consumers are modern and outwardly progressive. Their values are still Confucian but more and more an individualistic streak can be observed, bringing with it more progressive political opinions and expressions.

Lifestyle plays an important role in their value system, and an expression of success and wealth is allowed as long as it is not over-the-top. Family is important but more as a choice than a traditional burden.

Some markets (Hong Kong, Taiwan and Korea) display a deep uncertainty about their political future and this has had some 'slowing down' effect on consumers' material aspirations.

Women have taken on a more active and assertive role, and communications needs to reflect that change and be increasingly focused in addressing its targets. These women consumers appreciate sophisticated advertising, humour with a twist, high production values and intelligent messages.

4. The "I just want to enjoy life" markets of Australia and New Zealand

These markets, though obviously very developed, pride themselves in making very rational choices, being down to earth and not following every advertising fad. The ostentatious display of wealth is frowned upon.

Communication needs to be humorous and mirror the 'twinkle in the eye' and 'down to earth' self-positioning to be successful. These markets have also matured to a stage where they can laugh at themselves, and many advertising campaigns have successfully used this fact to reach out to their targets.

Based on the cultural clusters, we can then deduce guidelines for creative briefs that can be the basis for developing communication that is locally relevant, covers more than one market and thus minimises production costs, and still keeps the positioning of the brand consistent across the region. Furthermore, if the target group is young, it may even be possible to attempt to find the 'holy grail' in cross-cultural marketing, where the 'holy grail' refers to communication that is consistent, relevant and can work across all markets in Asia. For the most time, however, this will remain a marketer's dream.

I THIS AD
I THIS AD
I THIS AD
I THIS AD
I THIS AD
I THIS AD

이광고가
이광고가
이광고가
이광고가
이광고가
이광고가

I THIS AD
소방용품보관함
소방용품 보관함 사용방법

I THIS AD
갈아타
Transfer

I THIS AD

11. Responsible advertising

'How do you evaluate a TVC or any piece of communication or advertising'? In a class discussion, I told my students about Keith Reinhard's ROI (relevant, original, impactful) and added my own 'C' for credibility. A student from mainland China said, "Human values". At first, I did not know what to make of it. Human values? Someone volunteered a translation: Social responsibility. Are ads only good ads when they are socially responsible? I was ready to dismiss this thought as socialist propaganda. Isn't advertising all about selling products and positioning brands with the aim of making more profit?

Two things came to mind. One was Bill Bernbach's quote about our responsibility as advertisers. He said, "All of us who professionally use the mass media are the shapers of society. We can vulgarise that society. We can brutalise it. Or we can help lift it onto a higher level." We do not operate in a vacuum, therefore we need to be aware of the kind of message we are sending out in our communication. The other thing was that keeping human values and social responsibility in mind may actually be economically viable. Gone are the days when consumers merely wanted a good quality product at a low price and cared nothing about how and where it was produced, who produced it and under what conditions it was produced. Today, people have started to ask questions. This movement first began in the West but, more and more so, the questions are being asked here in Asia as well. Given this new customer awareness that is growing in Asia, it may make good business sense to look for messages of social responsibility when constructing advertising.

Going back to the film *Flashback* that I mentioned at the beginning of this book (starring a young Kiefer Sutherland and Dennis Hopper as an old 60s activist), the memories were of the 'summer of love', the 60s revolutionaries and their political heritage that made up the search for a better world and for new values. "There's a whole generation with a new explanation," so the song goes in Scott MacKenzie's *San Francisco* (1967). This "new explanation" was not only about peace, individual freedom and human rights, but also about responsibility and a questioning of the rat race and post-war consumerism. The wave swept the globe and was a dominant force for a while. Then, for a long time, it seemed that it was all forgotten.

In the 80s, greed was good. Gordon Gekko (corporate raider character in the 1987 Wall Street film) ruled the world, consumerism went unchallenged and companies produced in every way they could, never mind the human or natural environment. Bigger was better, and advertising showed this glitzy new world in commercials that cost millions. They showed "paradise on TV", as the German singer-songwriter Wolf Biermann put it in 1977. Of course the world suffered a rude awakening when oil prices went up, went down again, and then up again to stay up. The environment suffered badly. And people started to ask questions.

Fast forward to the end of 2008. We live in a new world, fundamentally changed by the Internet, with a more 'emancipated' consumer that no longer just cares about getting a good product at a low price. The new consumer is one who cares about who produces it, and how the company treats its staff and the environment.

These days, with an emancipated consumer who is much better informed and more critical, advertising has to change. It has to take into account the changed mindset, and develop a new honesty in advertising. It also has to work with the clients to make sure that their messages are not only truthful but still relevant to their target group. Since the target group may now be asking different questions, any communication must have answers to these questions in order for the brand to survive.

The emancipated consumer is also no longer a passive consumer. Communication has to change from being a monologue to becoming a dialogue. This can lead to a new area of content co-creation where advertisers allow their consumers to create their own ads by supplying the materials and tools.

But beware. You may not always like what you see. The Chevy 'Make your own Tahoe commercial' campaign didn't go as Chevrolet planned. Chevy Tahoe had invited consumers to create their own car ads online and many instead used the materials to create anti-car ads and warn against global warming. But co-creating content, if done right, can be an opportunity for companies to bond with consumers, to tap into their creativity and thus make the brand more real and approachable. Al Gore's 'Current TV' is based on that concept. Consumers upload news reports they have shot themselves onto the website, and a selection of those is broadcast on the cable channel.

This trend has inspired some new brands that fit into the niche—think Bodyshop, and all shops offering natural skin care, natural fabrics, and natural or organic food. This has forced other brands and companies to rethink the way they do business and to re-analyse their reputation and engage in activities that they had never thought of before.

Remember Faith Popcorn's "S.O.S. = Save Our Society"? Companies, and not just governments, are starting to care about social, environmental and developmental issues in a way that is meaningful and that instigates real change as opposed to the Benetton ads of the 80s and 90s that were out to shock but did not change behaviour.

And how is this relevant to branding and communication? Where branding is concerned, companies must revisit their core and see whether their brand and the way it is positioned and defined, has an element of responsibility and of caring as part of its DNA. That's because, sooner or later, consumers will start asking questions, and you'd better have some answers. An even better strategy would be to pre-empt those questions by determining what your brand stands for and communicating the message effectively.

In communication, it is not just the message and content that need to reflect the new values. We also need a new communication style. Over the years, consumers have become very, very and critical of traditional advertising. They don't believe the old-fashioned, 30-second commercial any more. They switch off, they don't care, and they use other media. Technology gives them the tools to filter out any undesired advertising messages and so communication today needs to use new channels to reach its targets. The message needs to reflect the increased consumer sensitivity regarding environmental and ethical issues, and companies need to engage consumers.

The New Media, mainly the Internet, has created a new type of consumer, one who is more active, more in control, more critical and better informed. Brands can make use of this channel and the new consumer mindset by actively engaging the consumer through communication that takes the viewer seriously and invites genuine feedback and participation. The fundamental difference about this new consumer is that, for the first time, he has a voice. She has a voice. And that voice will be heard, whether you like it or not. In blogs, forums and outdoor stickers in the streets of Berlin and Seoul, the voice of consumers is now engaging brands that advertise. It is giving feedback, telling them what they think and demanding better ads.

Companies can make use of this voice and invite active participation from their audience. If done right, the audience will respond and share their feelings and opinions. They are already doing it in millions of personal blogs, which in turn have become the most important, trusted source of information for buyers who are in the market—whether for a new stereo, a car or just a face-cream.

And thus, co-creation of content and the quest for more 'responsible' ads are here to stay.

PETER SMYTH

Friends of Jörg

Senior Strategist,
Strategic Planning Group,
I&S BBDO Inc.

The Way Of Japanese Advertising

"Just how long do you think you'd be staying in Japan?"

I was a bit surprised by the question.

I had recently moved to Tokyo as part of an international transfer within BBDO, my advertising agency of 10 years. I loved my new city, and I had decided to get more involved in the local culture. I had settled on studying Kyudo—Japanese archery. There was an elegance and simplicity in Kyudo that attracted me, and a physical aspect to the sport that looked like a fun challenge as well. Plus, getting a reputation as a guy proficient with powerful long-range weapons probably wouldn't hurt me in future conversations with my clients.

So I had started searching for places in Tokyo where I could study Kyudo. And, after finding a place and introducing myself to a sensei, I was asked that question—how long would I be in Japan?

I responded to the sensei that I planned to be in Tokyo for two or three years at least.

"*Soo desu ka…*", he replied thoughtfully, and sucked in some air through his teeth. "I should tell you that if you chose to study with us, you won't be picking up a bow until well into your second year."

"But what will I be doing until then?" I asked, a bit confused about how one studies archery without lifting a bow.

"Mainly learning how to breathe properly, how to sit, how to get up and hold yourself correctly. How to clear your mind. Along with other junior duties to the club. Only after you master those tasks will you actually receive your bow."

Whammo.

It seemed that, once again, I had run into an activity dictated by a Japanese 'Way'. There would be no picking up a bow and just firing off a few arrows—no 'beginner's luck' to see if I could hit the target. Rather, if I wanted to study under this sensei, I would have to approach my studies in an accepted and regimented way.

It was an experience I had run into before.

You can't move around in Japan without becoming acutely aware that there is almost always a proper way in which things are to be done. You approach business negotiations in a certain way, you wait on subway platforms in a particular way, and you even sort your garbage in a certain way.

Sociologists argue that the hundreds of hidden rules and processes in Japan arose from this being 'a high context culture'. Japan's high degree of homogeneity and shared culture allowed a deep context to develop around activities, where rules of behaviour became routine and unspoken. Simple things came to be wrapped with layers of shared meaning, often misunderstood by an outsider.

This high degree of homogeneity means that interactions and communication can be simple on the surface, yet subtle and layered underneath. And while a foreigner might miss the subtleties, most Japanese can easily understand them.

The idea of a simple idea conveying a deep meaning is illustrated by any one of the haiku poems from the Basho era (17th century), for instance:

Breaking the silence of an ancient pond,
A frog jumped in the water—
A deep resonance.

The mood and meaning of the short poem is felt through its words, rather than literally expressed. The words manage to create an almost visual scene where the mood 作法 (*sahou*) can be felt without a direct description.

Japanese advertising today is also heavily dependent on understanding and creating the right *sahou* around a product. Often, visually oriented,

Japanese advertising tends to be indirect in nature, evoking a particular mood or emotion.

Consequently, ad people expend a lot of effort in trying to create the right mood for our advertising. In a recent one-on-one interview with a consumer, we knew we had gotten it right when she said that she not only understood the message of our print ad, but she also described our work as having the right *sahou* too: "You can just see it (the message)—you don't even have to read it."

Because underlying rules are so important in Japan, really understanding the context and expectations surrounding Japanese advertising is hugely important before developing a campaign here. As a researcher friend of mine reminded me recently, while the reasons are not always immediately evident, there are really, really good reasons why Japanese advertising is done the way it is. Japanese ad guys know what they're doing and what works in this market to really sell their products.

It would be a mistake for a foreign marketer to come to Japan and conclude they could 'improve' the marketing, without first understanding the context surrounding their product, and the expectations Japanese have of their advertising. Like studying Kyudo, the development of advertising here follows rules. And it is important that we first really understand what lies behind the 'Way' of Japanese advertising. And only then can we start to improve upon it.

WHY I HATE CONSUMERS

Consumers.

I hate them.

Really, I do.

My job of understanding consumers would be so much easier if I didn't have to actually deal with the people.

After 10 years of studying consumers for my job at BBDO, a major international advertising agency, I've come to the rather scientific conclusion that no matter the international market and no matter the category, people are basically crazy. They're simply not rational, and they can never tell me the real reasons why they do the things they do.

Let me give you an example:

You decide to buy yourself a new laptop. You head into a local electronics store and, after shopping around, comparing prices and models, you settle on a nice little machine packed with all the features you need and it costs a reasonable US$1500. You're sold, and have the salesman get you the machine. But as you are happily standing in line waiting to pay, you start a conversation with another customer and discover that there's another store about 20 minutes away, offering the same exact laptop on sale for $15 less.

What do you do? Just buy the $1500 laptop now, or get into your car, drive for 20 minutes and get the $15 discount?

If you're like most people, you'll probably choose to just buy the laptop now.

But then imagine you are in this situation:

You decide to buy yourself a new calculator. You head into a local electronics store and, after shopping around, comparing prices and models, you settle on a nice little machine packed with all the features you need and it costs a reasonable US$30. You're sold, and have the salesman get you the machine. But as you are happily standing in line waiting to pay, you start a conversation with another customer and discover that there's another store about 20 minutes away, offering the same exact calculator on sale for $15 less.

What do you do? Just buy the $30 calculator now, or drive across town and get the $15 discount?

Most people will put the calculator down and pull out their car keys.

Of course, the kicker here is that it's exactly the same situation. For the exact same expenditure of time, you'll get $15 dollars. So why do so many people choose to just buy the laptop in the first store, but travel to the second store for the calculator?

Simple—people are not rational. Consumer behaviour is not driven simply by logic, but also by the context in which a situation or statement occurs.

Here's another example:

You're out on a Friday night and standing alone at a dark, hip bar, waiting for a friend to arrive. An attractive person slides up next to you, touches your arm, leans in closely, looks directly in your eyes and huskily whispers, "Could I trouble you for a light for my cigarette?"

Now, the rational person simply understands that this person's cigarette is unlit.

But for the rest of us, we'd start running through a million other scenarios in our minds—Is there more to this than this person simply needing a light? What does this person think of me? Do I like this person? What should I reply? What does this person really want? And so on.

Because people are complex and illogical, the message conveyed is never the only thing received. People are not blank slates, simply receiving messages that are sent to them. Those messages are always wrapped in layers of meaningful context. One of my favourite quotes comes from the Jewish Talmud, which states:

"We do not see things as they are; we see things as we are."

The thing I've learned is to never assume that the marketing message I am sending is the one that the consumer is receiving. I always strive to understand the issues that matter to my customers, so that I'll be better able to address their viewpoints and concerns in my communication.

And, above all, every time one of these illogical, irrational, and frankly crazy people start to get me down, I take a deep breath, and then try to remember—I'm probably just as crazy as they are.

LIFE, LIBERTY AND THE PURSUIT OF CUSTOMERS

On 1 July 2003, close to 500,000 people marched through the streets of Hong Kong. While their reasons for marching were varied—some were protesting at the inept handling of the SARS outbreak, others were fed up with more than six years of falling property prices—the catalyst for the protest was the proposed change to Hong Kong's 'Basic Law'. The proposed legislation, referred to at the time as 'Article 23', would roll back a number of basic freedoms —such as freedom of the press and freedom of association—and stated that anyone found guilty of acts of treason, sedition, secession or subversion against mainland China could be jailed for life.

The protest put considerable pressure on Tung Chee-Hwa, Hong Kong's

Chief Executive and Beijing's main deputy in Hong Kong at the time. At first, he watered down several of the more distasteful provisions of the bill, intent on still pushing it through the Hong Kong Legislature. However, the resignation of three close political allies forced him to shelve the bill, and shortly thereafter, Beijing replaced Mr Tung.

So what, if anything, does all of this have to do with marketing?

Well, to me, there was a very basic principle at work in Hong Kong on 1 July—a principle that underlies just about all modern marketing efforts. It was the principle of choice, and a belief that the people know best. All of those protesters were making the point that they wanted a say in the future of Hong Kong; that they wanted alternatives to what Tung and Beijing were proposing; that they wanted a choice.

Giving people choices is absolutely central to Western liberal democracy. Politically, people have the right to choose their leaders. And if those leaders don't measure up, the people have the right to demand better alternatives.

Really good marketing is also about the development of better alternatives—alternatives that meet and solve consumers' needs in newer and better ways. Products and services that come directly from the people's desires—from a particular insight into their unique needs—will always win out over solutions imposed from above.

However, there are lots of people who still look at things in the old way. On a recent trip to Shanghai, I went to the 'Super Brand Mall' in the Lujiazui financial district. The mall, like many things in China, is billed as one of the world's 'biggest'. It is a truly impressive building—covering an area of 240,000 square metres, the mall stretches several city blocks and boasts an impressive 13 storeys. It is a shining testament to Shanghai's capitalist culture.

Unfortunately, it also stands mostly empty. In great contrast to its sweeping corridors and its grand façade, very few businesses had actually set up inside the mall. And while it may have been an unusually quiet day when I visited, I didn't see many customers in there either. The developers followed a 'Field of Dreams' philosophy—"Build it and they will come". The problem is, it doesn't look like people are really that interested in what the mall has to offer.

The Super Brand Mall may yet be a huge success, but it is reflective of a trend that is common across all command-driven economies—supply is created independent of consumer demand. A lot of this is due to foreign investors eager to gain an early foothold in China's huge potential market. But there's more to it than that.

The economy in China is still a lot like its politics—driven and directed from the top. Without attention paid to the people's wishes, you sometimes end up with unrepresentative politicians and empty shopping malls.

But as marketers, we know that ignoring your customers' desires never works in the long term. Eventually, you'll end up with a backlog of inventory, empty shopping malls, and dissatisfied customers. The solution is to really listen to people, and to use their feedback to give them choices and alternatives. The better alternatives eventually win, and people become more satisfied as a result.

Which is all that those 500,000 people who marched through Hong Kong really wanted—they wanted to be listened to and to be given better choices. It was a lesson that Mr Tung learned too late.

PETER SMYTH

Friends of Jörg

Senior Strategist,
Strategic Planning Group, I&S BBDO Inc.

Peter is a graduate of the University of Toronto, Trinity College with degrees in International Relations, East Asian studies and Geography—degrees which have absolutely nothing whatsoever to do with advertising.

Before joining BBDO, Peter worked for four years as an investment banker on the trading desk of a major European bank—a job which has absolutely nothing whatsoever to do with advertising.

So it follows in 1999 that Peter would leave a fruitful career in investment banking to enter the world of—you guessed it—advertising.

Since joining BBDO in January 1999, Peter has worked in three separate BBDO offices: BBDO Toronto, BBDO Hong Kong, and now I&S BBDO in Tokyo. Peter has worked on a wide range of business, including helping to build the FedEx brand in Asia, developing strategies for Doritos in Canada, and most recently working to drive the Pfizer and Gillette business in Japan. In addition to client work, he also helped develop and standardise the strategic planning process for all of BBDO's offices in Asia, and was the representative for Asia for a number of BBDO Worldwide initiatives. Peter has also taught strategic marketing development at the Ontario College of Art in Toronto, the Chinese University of Hong Kong, and Sophia University in Tokyo.

Wow—has it been a year already? Feels like yesterday when we won the account. All my friends are so envious that I work with Happy Jelly. But it's hard work with little pay. That's why I've quit and will start working at MCB next week—as an Account Manager for double the pay! I am so happy! See you there!

Index

(Page references in **bold** denote charts/pictures.)